D0276693

WEIRWOLF

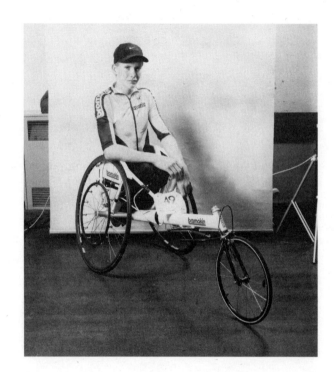

DAVID WEIR
WITH DAVID BOND
WEIRWOLF
MY STORY

Biteback Publishing

First published in Great Britain in 2013 by
Biteback Publishing Ltd
Westminster Tower
3 Albert Embankment
London SE1 7SP

Copyright © David Weir 2013

David Weir has asserted his right under the Copyright, Designs and Patents Act 1988 to be identified as the author of this work.

All rights reserved. No part of this publication may be reproduced, stored in a retrieval system or transmitted, in any form or by any means, without the publisher's prior permission in writing.

This book is sold subject to the condition that it shall not, by way of trade or otherwise, be lent, resold, hired out or otherwise circulated without the publisher's prior consent in any form of binding or cover other than that in which it is published and without a similar condition, including this condition, being imposed on the subsequent purchaser.

Every reasonable effort has been made to trace copyright holders of material reproduced in this book, but if any have been inadvertently overlooked the publishers would be glad to hear from them.

ISBN 978-1-84954-548-8

10 9 8 7 6 5 4 3 2 1

A CIP catalogue record for this book is available from the British Library.

Set in Sabon and Gotham

Printed and bound in Great Britain by
CPI Group (UK) Ltd, Croydon CR0 4YY

To Emily, Ronie, Mason, Tillia and Jenny

'Pity me not for my disabled state,
Nor think of me as less than what I wish to be,
My heart is beating now, at any rate,
And is a working part of who is me.'
Rachel Tyson

CONTENTS

FOREWORD BY
SEBASTIAN COE

London 2012 provided so many extraordinary moments and created so many heroes that it is almost invidious to focus on any individual athletes or their achievements. But David Weir's four gold medals must surely stand out as one of the outstanding performances in a truly astonishing summer.

There are many cherished memories I take with me from London and they will not dim with time. One of them is the wall of sound in the Olympic Stadium when David hit the home straight in the 5,000m. That was as loud as anything I heard during the Olympic Games or any other sporting event I have been to.

And I was there on the Mall when he powered his way to that fourth victory in the marathon. As a former middle-distance runner I marvelled at his physical ability to win over such a range of distances, and at the accompanying mental strength. To win the 800m, 1,500m, 5,000m *and* the marathon is pretty exceptional. But to do it in front of your home crowd in a home Games when the whole of the country is watching you and expecting you to deliver – well, that is unique.

I've sat with David after moments in his career when, by his own assessment, he has underperformed. It is to his eternal credit and the admiration of his peers that he has always regrouped and bounced back – but then David has the natural instinct of a winner, an ability to turn it on when it really counts. It is this quality that separates the good from the great, and David has it in spades.

Paralympic sport will never be the same again. Every day the Games set new records – whether for crowds, television audiences or for sheer spirit. In my closing ceremony address I spoke of how the Paralympians had lifted the cloud of limitation. No one summed that up better than David.

As with all the Paralympic athletes, he has not had it easy. As this book will show, he has been brave and honest about some of the challenges he has faced. But through sheer talent, hard work and determination he has not only overcome those challenges but managed to rise to the top of his sport.

His is a truly inspirational story.

DAVID WEIR
WEIRWOLF

CHAPTER 1

LET THE GAMES BEGIN

The routine is always the same.

I wheel my day chair – the one I spend most of my time in – alongside my racing chair. Using both my hands I push down to lift my body up before swinging my legs across onto the frame.

I drop one hip, easing between the wheels. My legs slide down into the cage, tailored exactly to my measurements, and then I tuck them tightly underneath me.

With my knees resting on a solid metal plate and my feet settling into their pod, I take two small straps – one over the top of my thighs and a second over the back of my ankles – and yank them tight.

Click, click, click.

I ratchet another padded strap firmly across the small of my back and the chair grips me. I try and move but can't. It's totally secure, man and machine made one.

Now, with my lower half locked into position, I lean forward at 45 degrees and stretch out my arms. From fingertip to fingertip my wingspan measures six foot two. It reminds me how tall I would be.

If I could stand.

With my arms stretched out I then lift my chin up and my head back, moving against the resistance created by my muscles. Until I hear it:

Crack.

I then squeeze my shoulder blades until I hear the same noise explode from my spine:

Snap.

Now I'm ready.

———

That morning I woke at eight. I tried to go back to sleep but it was no use. The adrenalin was already pumping. I lay there for an hour or so and then got up. I took a shower – in and out, no hanging around – and then flicked on the TV. I tried to do what I do every day. Problem was, this wasn't any other day. This was the moment I had been waiting for all my sporting life. From the moment London won the Olympics and Paralympics in Singapore in 2005, everything had been leading to this. I kept telling myself it was only the heats. Day one. No sweat.

It's funny how all the months of planning, the years of preparation suddenly feel woefully insufficient. I was in the best shape of my life but I still couldn't escape the nerves. Every time I glanced out the window of my apartment in the athletes' village I got a jolt, a reminder of the size of the task that lay ahead, all the pressure and expectation. Everywhere I looked, bright neon-pink and purple banners fluttered with the 2012 logo. The sun was shining and although it was early the crowds were already streaming onto the Olympic Park. The excited chatter of expectation drifted across the yawning expanse of this corner of east London. Here it was – London's Olympic and Paralympic dream made real. The curved roof of the Velodrome, shaped like a Pringle. The Aquatics Centre with those giant wings bolted onto the sides. The bubble-wrapped basketball venue, the Copper Box and, furthest away, the centrepiece – the Olympic Stadium itself. With its triangular-shaped floodlights perched on top of the roof it looked like a crown. For the next ten days this would be my stage. My home.

After the enormous success of the Olympics, everyone was wondering what the Paralympics would really be like. I kept reading about how the Paralympics was a sell-out, how there wouldn't be an empty seat in the house. Until I actually saw it I didn't want to believe it. I always hoped Britain and London would be different, that they would embrace us Paralympians. But I had been let down so many times in the past that I didn't want to get my hopes up. That morning, watching tens of thousands of people descending on the Olympic Park, I finally believed it. Now I couldn't wait for it all to start and to get in there and race. I just wanted to taste that atmosphere.

I had never enjoyed such a smooth ride into a major championships. There's normally something that goes wrong – illness, injury or problems at home. For the first time, everything was perfect, and I was itching to get on the track and prove myself. I also felt confident – something I wasn't used to feeling. That morning I bumped into Jonathan Edwards in the village. He would say to me later, after it was all over, that when he spoke to me he just knew I was going to do something special in the Games. He talked about a glow in my eyes and a level of physical fitness he just hadn't seen before.

At that point, though, all I was thinking about was whether I would be able to eat something. I hate eating on the day of big races. My stomach feels like a washing machine on the fastest possible spin cycle. You know you have to get something down to keep you going, but it's the last thing you want to do.

Feeling slightly peaky, I walked tentatively into the athletes' food hall. The scale of the place always takes my breath away. There's something here to tempt everyone – an aircraft hangar dedicated to the pleasure of eating. And top athletes need to eat a lot. It's open around the clock and can accommodate 5,000 hungry athletes in one sitting. There's a counter serving every type of food from every country imaginable. It's like one of those shopping centre food courts on steroids. At one end there's the giant, obligatory McDonald's (they are Olympic and Paralympic sponsors) – and although we are all supposed to be healthy-eating athletes, I was always surprised at how long the queues were!

This was no time for fast food, though. It would be hours until I raced my opening heat of the 5,000 metres so I needed to fill up on food with lots of energy. I ate a big bowl of muesli and then some bananas. There are always lots of bananas. I am also a big coffee drinker but it has to be dark and very, very strong. That's where McDonald's saved my life. Every morning during London, after I had eaten my breakfast I would head there for a double espresso. A lot of coffee lovers might find this hard to believe, but this was the only place on the Olympic Park where you could get a decent coffee. After the first, I would quickly follow up with a second to get the blood pumping.

I chatted to some of the other athletes as they ate their breakfast. I like to be around people. A bit of banter just helps take your mind off what's coming later in the day. If you are stuck in your room, you think too much and that can destroy you. I headed back to my apartment block and went upstairs to see some of the other lads, have a chat with the Welsh guys like Aled Davies. We would play some video games, chat and watch the telly. Anything to distract me.

I called my coach, Jenny Archer. We both knew I was ready but I still needed to hear it from her again. I have known Jenny since I was nine. She is my coach, my confidante, my psychologist, my second mum. She said the same thing she always says before big races.

'Do your own race, watch for crashes, watch for breaks and remember: stay out of trouble.'

I told her I was really nervous.

'But Dave,' she replied in that calming, measured tone she has. 'You're doing things I've never seen you do before. You've got nothing to worry about.'

My fiancée Emily was on the phone most of the time. She was also good at keeping me sane. She said, 'Just do your best.' I wanted to know what my little boy Mason was doing. He had just had his first birthday and even though the Games had only been under way for two days I had already been away for a while and was missing home. A bit of normality was exactly what I needed at that point.

My race wasn't until 7.30 p.m. So I knew I wouldn't be able to eat that night. That meant before too long I was back in the dining hall to have a big lunch – something healthy with loads of carbs. The problem for wheelchair racers is that once you are in your chair you are hunched down and everything gets very cramped. I find it incredibly uncomfortable. I have to eat at least three hours before a race. If I leave it too late I get heartburn or can't actually keep it down.

Then there's the beetroot juice – a whole litre of the stuff. The British team nutritionist had recommended it to me a year earlier. I couldn't believe the immediate impact it had on my performances. It just gave me so much energy. I know it sounds disgusting but it actually tastes OK. But you mustn't use it all the time otherwise your body becomes immune to it. So I just planned to use it for the Games, a litre a day for the three days before a final. I honestly don't think I could have contemplated going for four gold medals without the power of the beetroot.

I had already checked everything on my chair the night before but I still ran through it all again:

Bolts on the compensator (the device we use to direct the front wheel of our chairs during races)? Check.

Tyre pressure? Check.

Have I got my spare wheels for the track? Check.

I bundle up my little bag of tools, put on my Paralympics GB training top and head out of the apartment.

I got on the bus about 4.30 p.m. As it looped its way around the Olympic Park, past the Aquatics Centre, I rang Emily again.

'Love, I'm absolutely bricking it,' I told her.

I would like to have put it less bluntly but there was no getting away from the immensity of what was happening. This was the biggest time of my sporting career and I didn't want anything to go wrong. I started to heave but I couldn't actually be sick. My heart was pounding in my chest. I just wanted to get this heat out of the way and get to the final. Emily wished me luck and told me to just do my best. But what if my best wasn't good enough? What if, what if?

I headed for the warm-up track. I always like to get there early to check out who's at the British tent and to have a chat with some of the physios and doctors. I went to the toilet. A lot.

You see, once you are in your chair that's it. You can't go again until after you've raced and that can be more than three hours. It's a hell of a long wait. That's why I try to limit the amount of liquid I drink, but of course you have to be hydrated. It's a real catch-22. Throw in nerves and I might as well just warm up in the loo.

Once I am strapped in my racing chair and have gone through the process of clicking my back and neck, I tape up my fingers with Elastoplast – it helps stop the blisters you get from hammering the push rims on the chair. It takes about five minutes and while I am winding the tape around and around and cutting it with my teeth I keep a watchful eye on that warm-up track. Who's coming on, who's hanging back? Which athletes are out early? I watch everything. I never rush onto the track. I like to try and psyche my rivals out.

I have another shot of beetroot and then I push myself onto the circuit. At first it's just a steady eight to twelve laps. Maybe a few bursts of speed. I like to see who else is training and then I might go and sit behind them. Just to let them know I'm there. I really wanted to find Marcel Hug. A few years younger than me, he was one of my biggest rivals for gold. We race each other all the time. But on the warm-up track he always tries to avoid me. He doesn't want to get involved in my mind games.

As I go round and round, the adrenalin is really starting to pump. I feel good. Off in the distance I can hear the roars from the stadium. Now I want this to happen. Now the nerves are starting to fall away.

Chantal Petitclerc is keeping an eye on the time for me. She knows what this feels like. Chantal won fourteen Paralympic gold medals in four Games for Canada and now she is here working with Paralympics GB as a mentor for the team. She gives me a ten-minute reminder. I drink some water and do a few more laps. Then five minutes. Bit more water, last few laps. Then the race is finally called. An announcer tells all the athletes for the T54 5,000m to group together at the side of the warm-up track. We are then led across to the stadium.

We wheel our way towards a long, covered tunnel that will take us across one of the various rivers encircling the island on which London's shiny new Olympic Stadium sits. As we get closer I try and take it all in. The stadium reminds me of a spaceship. Above a section of the roof I see those unmistakable triangular floodlights and the giant screens showing the Paralympic flame burning. Multi-coloured lights are being projected on the huge wrap which covers the sides, throbbing and pulsing along with the noise of the crowd. It's electric.

When the stadium was still being finished, I remember mentioning the need to make sure the entry tunnel to the stadium was covered. I think it was raining that day and I was probably thinking about the unreliable British summer but I was also thinking ahead to this moment. I knew then that I would want to slip into the stadium anonymously. I didn't want anyone to see me before I got on the track. It would only add to the pressure on my shoulders.

Now we're deep under the stadium next to the indoor warm-up track. Some of my rivals take the opportunity to fine-tune their preparations, one last chance to get the muscles working. But I don't bother. I just sit there and wait. An official checks my bag, makes sure I haven't got anything I shouldn't have. No phone or iPod. I just have my bag of tools and some water. I go through my bag and pull out my tube of Glister – a glue I use to give extra traction on the push rims on the wheels of my chair. Rugby players use it too. Just to get a bit more grip.

At this stage you can't really tell what's going on above you. You can hear a few muffled cheers but you could be in a car park. Then a volunteer appears, carrying a wooden placard with our heat on it. We follow her back onto the concourse in the bowels of the stadium and around to where we go in. Now you can really hear the atmosphere. You can feel the noise.

This is it now. This is what I've dreamed of for so long. I close my eyes. I don't want to look. Then I do it. I open them as wide as I can, drinking it all in. From where we are positioned you can't see the crowd properly but it's incredible. A sea of faces, all blurred and bunched tightly together. It's packed. And so loud. At this point I am doing my best not to start blubbing. I just feel so proud. The fears fall away.

Whatever happened to me over the next few days, London and my country had done it. My worst nightmare was always that afterwards people would come up to me and say that the Games were rubbish. That Britain didn't deliver. I felt responsible. I know it sounds crazy, but that's how I felt. But opening my eyes, a few moments before my first race, reassured me. We weren't going to fail. This was going to be very special.

CHAPTER 2

WHY ME?

Cripple. That was the word that really used to get to me. I could take a lot of the insults. But cripple? That was just demeaning. That's the one that made me snap.

To this day I still don't know why I can't move my legs. As a child I would cry at night, asking over and over again: why me? I never let my parents hear. They wouldn't have put up with me being soft. They always taught me to just get on with things. They treated me like a normal kid and that's probably why I am the way I am today. I long ago learned to accept my disability. It's part of me and, although many people might find this difficult to understand, I don't ask why any more.

My mum is a strong woman. She takes everything in her stride. She decided very early on that I shouldn't just sit around, feeling sorry for myself. She says she could always sense something was not quite right when she was carrying me. But in the 1970s, pregnant women didn't get all the usual ultrasound scans that are commonplace today.

The doctors only did that if they thought there was something wrong. And no one did – so my mum just took their word for it and carried on. The only time the medics clocked there might be a problem was when she went into labour. She had been pushing for hours but nothing was happening. She kept telling the nurses something was wrong but they were too junior to make a decision. They just wouldn't listen. My mum knew that no matter how hard she pushed I wasn't coming out. She was terrified and thought both of us would die there and then in the ward. Eventually she started making a proper scene and a senior sister came to see her. She checked the bump and realised there was in fact a serious, serious problem and before my mum knew what was going on she had been whisked into theatre for an emergency Caesarean.

I was born on 5 June 1979 at St Helier Hospital in Carshalton, Sutton. But while my mother and father, Jackie and David, were relieved and happy, it had been a horrible experience and it was clear there were still major problems to deal with. Although the delivery was eventually a success the doctors discovered that the tops of my thighs were broken and badly misshapen. I also had club feet, or talipes, a condition where the feet are so twisted that the toes actually face each other. It's quite common and can be treated easily by putting a baby's legs in heavy plaster but it was obviously a very nasty shock for everyone.

It turns out that instead of my head pointing down in the

engaged position, I was folded in half and sitting across the width of my mum's belly, with my bottom on the left-hand side and my head on the right. After I was born, you could see the creases in my legs – like a line in a folded piece of paper. And because my head was in the wrong position, when they cut through the lining of my mum's stomach it wasn't where they expected it to be. They had to quickly move my mum's bowels and bladder out the way to get to me in time. It was very touch and go.

For the first few days after my arrival my mum was in agony. She couldn't even talk, her stomach hurt so much. But again, being the tough woman she is, she refused to lie around in bed and after a few days climbed out of bed to wash herself, put on some make-up and prove she could get back on her feet. The nurses gave her a round of applause. There was no way she should have been out of bed at that point but it told everyone, especially my worried dad, that she was going to be OK.

After a few more days' rest the doctors sent us home with my legs all plastered up, but it was another two weeks before the alarm bells really started ringing. My mum had a friend whose little girl had also been born with club feet. Mum popped around to her house to see her daughter and compare notes but noticed that underneath those plasters her feet and legs were still wriggling and moving. From day one, mine didn't move.

She rushed home crying and, in a blind panic, called the hospital. A nurse told her to calm down and reassured her that nothing was wrong. But from that moment she knew. She tells me she just had a feeling I would never be able to walk. She wishes she had listened to her intuition during the pregnancy but all the medical staff, the nurses and midwives, dismissed her concerns. And if they were sure it was all right, well, it was all right. Wasn't it?

Over the next few weeks my little body was subjected to test after test. I was taken to Queen Mary's Hospital, not too far from where we lived, and then eventually up to Great Ormond Street. Here, the doctors put my broken legs in traction and they discovered I had a condition known as spinal cord transection. It meant that the two nerves in my spine which give the lower half of my body movement and feeling had been impaired or damaged beyond repair. I was about six weeks old and completely oblivious to the bombshell, which the specialists had just delivered to my mum and dad. I would never walk, they said. The best I could hope for was to be able to bend down from a wheel-chair and pick up objects from the ground.

My mum cried all the way home on the bus. When she got back to the estate she spotted another little boy who lived near to us who has spina bifida. That's often confused with my condition but it's different as it has a clear cause – a hole in the spine. There was nothing like that in my case, there were no clues or explanation as to why I couldn't move my legs. When my mum saw this little boy she says she had a moment of clarity. She stopped crying and said to herself that she wasn't going to accept the situation. From that moment on she wasn't going to be beaten and was determined to treat me as normally as possible.

In the weeks ahead the doctors became more and more puzzled about my case. What was strange was that while I wasn't able to move my legs I had feeling in them. This was extremely unusual as normally victims of spinal cord transection are paralysed from the waist down. If they can't move, they can't feel. But I could. My mum used to tickle my legs and I would react. At one point the doctors were so convinced that I couldn't have feeling without movement that they threatened to pull one of my toenails out without any anaesthetic. My dad went mad and stepped in, telling them they had to stop. Eventually they believed him. But it just tells you how unusual my case is. I was in nappies until the age of seven but from very early on it was obvious I was in control of my bladder and could pee like anyone else. Most paralysed people need to wear a bag for their whole lives, but I can tell when I need to go. It gives me a great sense of independence and means I am able to live a pretty normal life with no one clearing up after me.

Lots of people said my parents should have sued the hospital. At one stage they thought maybe my spine had been broken during the delivery but no one could prove it, so what was the point? Maybe it was just one of those things. That was their attitude and as time went on and I grew older it rubbed off on me.

There is one strange story, though, which might offer an explanation. My mum tells me that when I started talking I used to freak her out by pointing to the clouds and saying I had another mummy and daddy who were killed and that I had been shot in the back and fallen off a horse into water. Apparently I used to repeat this little story again and again without any prompting. I was only two or three so you can imagine how weird this must have sounded. Maybe I had come back into this world too soon. Who knows? I am not a spiritual person at all (I don't believe in God because if there is a God how can you explain why people are born disabled?) but my mum is not as cynical as me. She has often retold that story, saying that it might explain why I am disabled. Perhaps it's just one of those little tales parents tell you to give you something to cling to.

My dad, nicknamed Sammy, is the strong, silent type. He was born in Northern Ireland, so perhaps living through the Troubles and then serving in the Irish Guards for so many years he just got used to getting on with things. But my elder brothers Alan, Paul and Tony found the fact I would never walk extremely hard to take. Alan, who is now fifty and lives in Western Australia, and my third brother Tony were both very good boxers. Paul is mentally impaired and still lives close to us on the estate, so my mum can keep an eye on him. Although they have a different dad to me, we are close and they are very protective of their younger brother.

For a long time it was difficult for my family and the doctors to assess just how badly impaired I was going to be. Until I started to try to walk there was no way of knowing what we were dealing with. Like any baby, as I got older I started to crawl. According to my mum and dad I had movement from the hips down – again, this was highly unusual for someone with my condition – and I could move the top of my knees. So that was how I first started moving around. I was so determined that I would just drag my legs behind me. For a while my parents must have had the faint hope that the doctors had got their diagnosis wrong. But once I was ready to walk it became clear that I was not going to miraculously recover. So instead I was trained to use these fierce-looking supports called callipers. They were made of metal with leather straps which went over my knees and the top of my thighs and then over my ankle. At the end of the calliper was a metal socket, which then sat inside the special hospital shoes I had to wear. In the early years I didn't mind them too much – even the shoes, which were really hideous. But as I got older and more streetwise I started to hate the way they looked. They made me stand out and so I used to adapt pairs of trainers so I fitted in. You know what kids are like at school with trainers. As long as you didn't go for the really fancy Nike Air brands with the bubbles in the soles then you could cut the bottoms off and make them work. That made me feel a lot better and gave me street cred with the older kids, who I wanted to impress. The callipers were also good for keeping my legs and feet straight, which you obviously can't do in a wheelchair, and I stayed in them until I was eleven or twelve. I can't say I looked after them very much. We were always up the hospital picking up replacements. I was forever jumping out of trees or throwing myself about. I didn't care that they were made of steel and I developed a way of moving on them really fast by planting them down and swinging through the middle. It wasn't what most people did but even in those early days it was obvious I was prepared to adapt whatever support I was given in the search for speed.

———

I grew up on the Roundshaw Estate in Wallington. Built in the mid-1960s, it's the usual mix of high-rise flats and prefab houses. We were in one of the houses, although we called them decks because they were all linked together by an upper walkway. They were really maisonettes built around an internal ring road. You were physically shielded from the outside world and it created a great sense of community and togetherness. It was fantastic for the initial wave of tenants when they were first built. It's had quite a spruce-up in the last ten years or so but by the time I was born it had become quite badly run down. It had actu-ally been built on part of the land which formed the old Croydon Airport in the 1930s. But in the years after the war it had become a wasteland and so was developed in the 1960s for social housing. Tell most people you live in Wallington and they will have images of the leafy Surrey stockbroker belt. But Roundshaw was different, a sort of no man's land sandwiched uneasily between Croydon's outer London urban sprawl and the comfy, middle-class suburbia of Sutton. Even today it has a bad reputation – mainly for drugs and gangs of kids causing trouble. They pulled the high-rise flats down shortly after 2000 and that has improved the place a lot. It had become very shabby and the police were always around, stopping people and asking questions.

Because it had no main roads running through it, it always felt very secure to me. Yes, there were some hard people living there. But for me it's always felt safe and I still live there to this day. Even Paul is able to look after himself in his own flat just around the corner.

My mum moved to Roundshaw from Pimlico with her first husband, Derek, a technician for the London Electricity Board, in 1970. Alan and Paul had already come along and by then my mum was carrying Tony. The flat they had in Pimlico was in a brilliant location. It was on a huge estate called Churchill Gardens, right next to the River Thames, close to Victoria and the West End. But, as was quite common in those days, it was in the name of her mum, and my gran, Gladys. For years my gran worked for the Treasury Solicitors' office, which was nearby. But now, with two kids and a third on the way, the flat was way too small.

It was Derek's mother who first made the move out to Wallington. She had heard about the new estate being built and had managed to secure one of the maisonettes. She urged Mum to do the same but at first my mum was a bit reluctant. She had been told there was an airport nearby and she didn't fancy the noise of planes taking off and landing. She didn't realise the airport had been shut for years. Once they saw it, they thought it was perfect for raising a growing family. So they put their name down with the council for a move.

But the change of scene and the arrival of Tony wasn't enough to keep my mum and Derek together, and after fifteen years they split up. My mum says it was because they got together and had kids too young. It seems they just drifted apart. He still lives in the area and they are good friends. Soon afterwards my mum was introduced to David, my dad. His nickname, Sammy, had stuck from his army days – apparently there were so many people called David in his regiment that they needed to find a name to distinguish him from all the others. He joined up when he was seventeen. He was sent on tours all around the world and used to tell me stories of fascinating places like Belize and China. I never imagined that when I was older I would serve my country in my own way.

Judging by some of his stories, my dad must have been super-fit during his time in the army. One day, during his tour to Belize, he was getting pissed in a bar with some of his mates. It had been a long, boozy session and they were totally out of it when the drill sergeant burst in and told them to run a mile there and then. My dad says he was so drunk he could hardly walk and the heat was suffocating. But he had no choice. So he ran the mile. When he came back the sergeant checked his heart rate. It was basically normal. The sergeant refused to believe he had run anywhere. So he made him run it again. Afterwards he took his heart rate again and the same thing happened. It was as if he hadn't run anywhere. It must be in my genes because I have exactly the same ability to recover – no matter how gruelling the race.

After the army he became a builder and Mum worked full time for Philips, the electronics company, which was based in Croydon. She used to arrange for technicians to go out to people's houses and fix their washing machines. She worked all the time up until her retirement. She was so determined to give all of us the best chance in life and I am so grateful for her and Dad's support. It can't have been easy with a son in a wheelchair trying to conquer the world.

From the start, though, it was clear it was going to be hard going. They never accepted people telling me I couldn't do things and that has been such a major influence on the way I perceive the world. The first time I was taken to the local play centre, the woman who ran it (she's still there today, incidentally) refused to let me join in at first because she insisted I would endanger myself and others. My mum went nuts and told her exactly what she thought of that. She, rightly, pointed out that it was no different if I fell off a climbing frame and had to go to hospital than if an able-bodied child did the same thing. After a while the woman backed down and let me join in. I spent most of my summers down there and in the end it was like that stand-off had never happened. But it was an important lesson very early on that I was going to meet plenty of hardened attitudes and hurdles along the way in life.

But in those days I simply didn't feel different and in many ways I'm exactly the same now. As far as I was concerned then, I was just like any other kid. And all I wanted to do was copy my friends – run around, kick a football, ride a bike. I wasn't going to let my disability hold me back.

To make sure I didn't feel left out, my parents had a special bike made for me. It was a clunky three-wheeler which I could pedal with my hands. It worked just like a normal bike except the pedals were where the handlebars were and the crank and chain ran down to the front wheel, which drove the machine forward. I remember it had a red frame with one wheel at the front and two big white wheels at the back with massive mudguards. It was so big you could probably have fitted two people on the back. Once I got that, whoosh, I was off, charging around with my mates, who all had the latest BMXs. I didn't care, it just made me feel part of the gang.

We would set up ramps using old sheets of wood and bricks lying around in the woods near the old airfield strip at the back of the estate. I would always be the first one to try them out. I had absolutely no fear of coming off. Mind you, most of the time I wasn't going very fast. My trike was so heavy that my mates had to push me to get me going.

Once, though, when I was about ten, we got the courage to go a bit further than usual. We constructed this really big jump at the bottom of a hill. My heart was pounding in my chest as I got ready to go for it. I look at the hill now and think it's just a little bump but at the time it felt like a mountain.

My friends gave me a shove to get me started.

'I've bitten off too much here,' I thought as my three wheels began to gather pace, heading towards this rickety-looking ramp we had built at the bottom. I slammed into the plank and took off. It felt like I was flying for ages before I crashed down to earth with a hell of a bump. I wobbled from side to side before getting my balance again, just managing to wrestle back control in time to avoid the trunk of a massive old tree. All my mates cheered.

If I wasn't on my bike, then I would be on my skateboard. I would just sit on it and use my hands to propel me forward. I loved it. The only problem was I used to get blisters on my hands from pushing against the hard ground – a sign of things to come.

Football was really my dream and I didn't want anything to stop me. We had a patch of grass just around the back of the house and that's where we played all the time. I would go in goal, sit on the floor and use my callipers to try and block the ball. I became quite a good keeper although the imaginary crossbar between the two jumpers was set a bit lower for me because the other kids knew that I couldn't stand or jump around. They used to smash the ball at me as if I was just like the rest of the kids. I liked that. I just wanted to get on with things. Deep down, though, I envied that they were able to run around and kick the ball, dribble and score goals. That was all I dreamed of and I used to spend a lot of time watching my team, Arsenal, on the TV, imagining myself doing the things all the top players could do.

We didn't go on many holidays as a family when I was a kid. Maybe it was because my parents didn't have loads of money or perhaps it was just too much hassle transporting a disabled kid everywhere. But the one that sticks in my mind was a trip to Cornwall when I was about seven. We must have stayed at a holiday camp because there were all these redcoats around. The car journey in our white Mini Metro seemed to go on for ages; it was the furthest I had ever been. I think my mum was worried her car would burn out. Once we were there I had a fantastic time, especially when I went swimming with my dad. He was a good swimmer and he could do the butterfly, which I was so impressed by. I could already swim a bit but it was so magical being taught to swim by my dad properly, being shown how to do the front crawl. I can still feel the chlorine from that pool stinging my eyes. We spent so much time in there. In fact, my parents had to buy me some eyewash to help my eyes – they were so red. The weather was scorching hot and we went to the beach a lot. My dad bought me a tiny dinghy. He would pull me out on the string and I would float around. It was such a fantastic holiday – maybe all the more memorable because we didn't do it very often. We never went abroad because my mum hates flying. A lot of my summer holidays were spent on Roundshaw.

I didn't mind that too much. It was a great place to play around and explore and every day seemed to bring a different adventure. I was also lucky to have such a tight group of friends, and two brothers who were handy in the boxing ring. Without that it might have been different but whenever I got into fights they stepped in to sort it out. It was only when I ventured off the estate that I encountered problems.

Most of the time, I just ignored the abuse. Kids can be cruel and my parents always told me to be strong and that other people would try and wind me up and make me feel bad. But occasionally the abuse would hurt. It would hit home.

When I was about fifteen I started seeing a girl in Croydon. She went to a school a couple of miles away and moved in totally different circles. For reasons I will never understand, her friends obviously saw me as a threat. One day I got a call from her number. But it wasn't her. A few of her schoolmates had got hold of her phone and rung my number. I answered.

'Hello?'

'Is that Dave?'

'Yeah, what do you want?'

'If you keep hanging around, we are going to take you out to the desert and leave you there without your crutches or your chair.'

Then they just hung up. How vicious is that? What sort of nasty person would dream of saying that sort of thing?

I cried a lot after that. But as time went on and I grew older I realised it was exactly that sort of cruelty that made me even more determined to prove that I wasn't going to be held back. That I couldn't just be equal to other people. I could be even better.

CHAPTER 3

I DON'T FEEL DISABLED

School should have felt like home. After all, every kid at Bedelsford, a special school for children with disabilities in Kingston upon Thames, had one kind of problem or another. Whether it was mental or physical, we were all lumped together, the outcasts, all of us trying to make the best of it. I suppose it should have created a greater sense of togetherness, a closer bond brought about by bad luck. Whatever insults you got from people on the outside, Bedelsford was a sanctuary, a place where we all could stick together.

The problem was, I didn't feel like the others. I didn't feel disabled. I know that will sound weird to people who are able bodied. I can hear them asking themselves whether I have looked in the mirror lately. But I have never really accepted it.

Maybe it's because I grew up on the Roundshaw Estate, where all my mates treated me as one of them. Maybe it's because my mum and dad never made excuses for me. They expected me to fend for myself as much as possible, even from an early age. I always tried to think as an able-bodied person would. I have never had any changes made to the houses or flats I have lived in to accommodate my chair. I have adapted to the houses, not the other way around. It has always been about creating a sense of normality. And I think that's what has made me so strong – so determined to prove people wrong.

But at school, that just made me feel more alone. I tried to talk to the other kids but I felt distant from them. And maybe that's why, when I look back, school didn't feel like a happy experience for me. I never told my mum how I felt. I didn't have the bottle. By the time I plucked up the courage to say something to her it was almost time to leave. All I wanted was to go to a mainstream school with my friends. But she knew I would just get into trouble. All I know is that I would have been much happier. I don't blame my parents for that – they were just looking after me. Trying to do their best.

As I got a bit older I did get a taste of what it might be like in a 'normal' school. A group of five or six of us were taken for lessons at Tolworth Girls' School, a mainstream comprehensive just up the road from Kingston. That made me feel a little less cut off. But in another sense it also reminded me of what I wasn't able to do. It was a terrible system for mildly disabled people like me.

Had I been going to school today I would have had a very different experience. Thanks to the Equality Act I would be integrated into a mainstream school. There would be no feeling of segregation, of being shut away from the rest of society. Having separate schools, well meaning though they might have been at the time, only reinforced the differences. Is it any wonder it's so hard to close the gap in the workplace once disabled children leave school and go out into the real world?

There's no doubt things have changed. Kids don't stare at you now. Whenever I left the refuge of Roundshaw I would have the piss taken out of me. I tried to put it out of my mind, to channel it in a way that made me stronger. I was always trying to test myself, to prove I was normal. About two miles down the road from my house there's a leisure centre called Westcroft. It's a decent walk for most people but for someone on callipers it's like a marathon. Not for me. After a few years of getting around on these things I had developed quite a technique and it didn't take me long to cover those two miles. I would get some very strange looks from people as I trundled along, slamming the crutches down and then pivoting my legs and body through the middle, a bit like a gymnast on the parallel bars. But by that point I didn't give a stuff about what people thought. This was how I got around and they should just mind their own business.

Sometimes when I travel abroad I get that sort of attitude. There are some parts of the world where they are simply not used to seeing people with disabilities out in public doing everyday things. I have learned to expect it and now just turn the other cheek. In Britain these days, I rarely get that awful feeling that someone is shocked or scared by what they are seeing. People just accept it. I noticed things changing about a decade ago – the country seemed to be getting more open, more tolerant. Of course there are still idiots about. Take the shocking example of the parents who left abusive messages for the one-armed children's TV presenter Cerrie Burnell on a BBC website. They complained to the BBC that she was scaring children with her appearance. I felt really sorry for her, she didn't deserve that. But my experience of most kids now is that they aren't as shocked or scared of people with disability as some adults are. Because schools are so integrated now, with disabled and able-bodied children grouped together, it's not such a big deal. As a result there doesn't seem to be the same vindictiveness. Of course children will always say nasty things to each other – they don't understand what they are really saying. But when I speak to my ten-year-old daughter Ronie about it she says it just isn't an issue and that her mates never take the mickey out of her because her dad's in a chair. She might just be saying that to protect her dad, I suppose. But I don't think so. I think it has changed dramatically. I just wish it had happened sooner, so I could have experienced school without that division.

In the beginning, going to Bedelsford didn't bother me. I didn't know any different. It was only when I got a bit older and started to get a bit streetwise that I realised I shouldn't be there. By the time I was eleven it really hit home, especially when my mates started going to big secondary schools. They seemed to be having such a laugh, meeting girls, making new friends. And there I was, being picked up and driven to my 'special' school in Kingston. When I look back now I think that's probably one of the reasons why I just didn't learn. It wasn't the school's fault. It was a good place and all the teachers there really helped me. And I never missed a day unless I was ill or had a hospital appointment. My mum wouldn't have let me.

Getting there was a bit of a drag. It's a fair old journey to Kingston from Wallington in rush-hour traffic. Some days it could take almost an hour. In the early days I was picked up in a bus provided by the council. Then I had a driver of my own called George. He was a lovely man. We used to talk about the estate and all sorts of stuff. That always used to cheer me up. Having someone familiar and friendly to talk to was a bit of a release from home.

But the truth is I just didn't want to go there, and I couldn't talk to my mum about things like that because she would have just batted it away, saying, 'You have to go. It's good for you.'

She didn't understand back then that I just didn't belong. That I was trapped in an awkward place – not so disabled that I needed 24-hour support and care but unable to get around without my chair or my callipers.

I wasn't very academic. I liked history – I loved learning about the kings and queens of England. I also liked geography and as I have got older I have become a bit of a map bore. I love nothing more than spending time studying Google Maps. I am just fascinated by them and can spend hours looking at different places. But the school stopped both history and geography for reasons I never did understand. As for everything else? I simply wasn't interested. Religious education, I couldn't stand. Maths, I was just about OK, while I only liked science if it was practical, which normally meant burning things. As for English, the less said about that, the better. How my teachers would laugh at the idea of me writing my own book. A lot of them thought I was good in class and worked hard but they would get frustrated because I didn't do enough homework. I should have listened to them and knuckled down. It is one of my big regrets that I didn't work harder at school and get a better education.

Although Bedelsford is now mainly dedicated to disabled children with speech and severe learning difficulties, when I went it was a mix. That meant the school was dealing with a whole range of needs and challenges. A lot of the physically impaired kids were actually very brainy. In that sense it was just like any other school, with some kids brighter than others. I always felt the other children were a bit innocent, though – like they had been wrapped up in cotton wool by their parents. As a dad I now totally understand. But back then I couldn't get my head around it at all. When I was fourteen or fifteen I started going to raves. When I went in on Monday morning and some of them asked what

I had got up to over the weekend and I told them, a lot of them would look mystified.

'What's a rave, Dave?'

They just didn't know. They were a bit naive. One kid couldn't even dress himself. But he was just like me. Why couldn't he get himself ready in the morning?

I don't want to give the impression that my school days were all bad. They weren't. And without Bedelsford I wouldn't have got into sport and I wouldn't have become a wheelchair racer. I might have hated going to school and studying, but I can't thank them enough for helping put me on the path to a life in sport.

While the rest of the lessons were a chore, I absolutely lived for PE. I couldn't wait for Friday afternoons, when the classes were held. My PE teacher, Julie Wrathall, was a very good hockey player and used to encourage me to play as many sports as possible – hockey, rugby, different forms of athletics. I even played tennis against Sir Cliff Richard when he came to visit the school one day (he didn't play in a wheelchair). Even when the PE lessons weren't on I was always trying to organise the other kids to play some sport or other in the playground during breaks.

But by the time I was eight, sport had already become a central part of my life. Even at that stage I was training two or three times a week. It was around that time that the school offered me my first real taste of competition. One of the physios who worked at the school had seen how keen I was on sport and asked me if I would like to do the London Mini-Marathon. They explained it was like the London Marathon but over a much shorter distance. At that time the marathon was one of the only sporting events on TV where you could watch disabled people competing. It was only for a few moments every year but I remember watching it and thinking, 'I would love to do that.' Now I was being offered the chance to actually do it – although I had to get through the trials first. So, four months before the race I had to show I was good enough by doing a two-mile race in a crappy little hospital chair. It was a bit of a rough course – it took you along public paths and up and down kerbs. The target was to complete the course in less than thirty minutes. I scraped through. Just.

At the same time as all this was happening, I was also playing basketball. I was just looking around to see which sport was best for me. Obviously I couldn't play football or take up boxing so I had to find something that would stimulate me. Basketball was one of the first things I wanted to do. Gordon Perry, the first man to win the wheelchair marathon, was a coach for the under-18s Great Britain basketball team and he was always trying to convert me. I even competed for my country as a junior in a multi-sport event in Australia. Although I was there first and foremost as a wheelchair racer, Gordon asked me to step in for one match to give some of the other players a rest. I loved it and we won comfortably.

But racing gave me that extra buzz. It might be because

it's an individual sport. I used to get frustrated on the basketball court if some players weren't playing to their potential or pulling their weight. If I lose a race then it's my fault – I can't blame anyone else. So as time went on I devoted myself more and more to athletics.

I don't even recall where I finished in that first mini-marathon – it can't have been anywhere near the front. But it gave me a real taste for the sport. It also helped me get picked for the London Youth Games – a competition which would come to be one of the defining moments of my young sporting life. Although Wallington is in the London Borough of Sutton I was actually approached by a coach and teacher from the neighbouring borough of Merton. It caused a bit of controversy at the time but the coach in question had spotted something special and wasn't afraid to ruffle a few feathers if it meant she got the best team. Her name was Jenny Archer.

Jenny was in her early forties when we first met. Stocky, with short blonde hair brushed back, she was both friendly and imposing at the same time. She had a warm smile but when cross her eyes could narrow, sending a shiver down your spine. It was a look which told you: 'Don't even try it.' Because of that, some people are scared of her and there's no doubt she can be tough. But she can also be very soft and, for me, she is like a second mother. My mum has never minded me saying that – they get on so well and she knows that Jenny would do anything to help me. It's weird but I probably see her more than I see my mum.

I won the 100m at the London Games that year and I will always remember what Jenny told me afterwards: 'You are a natural athlete,' she said, my mum and dad beaming away behind me. 'You've really got something. The way you move, the way you are built, the technique and power. It's all there. I know you are really young, Dave, but I am sure you could go on and be really special.'

My head was spinning. I could see my parents were struggling to take it all in.

'But the most important thing you have got is determination. The will to win. I can see it on that start line. Beating everyone else is what drives you on and that is more important than technique or natural athletic ability. Without that desire it's not even worth it. But you have got it. Now you have to work really hard to make sure you get the most out of your talent.'

Most kids aged eight might have found that overwhelming. I didn't. I felt special and it made me even more determined to compete and to keep getting better. People often talk about the moment they were inspired to go on and find the thing which defines them. For me, that was the moment.

Ironically, after that initial meeting, it would be another seventeen years before Jenny really played a central part in my life. In those days she was too busy with her career in football to devote the time to young athletes like me. She set me off on the road to becoming an athlete by introducing me to a training group at the Tooting Bec athletics track in Wandsworth and then went off to pursue her own sporting dream.

A decent athlete herself, Jenny ran the 400 metres and competed at international B level. But it was her time with Wimbledon Football Club that really made Jenny's name. She spent ten years with the so-called 'Crazy Gang' as a physio and rehabilitation coach. At first you wouldn't expect football hard men like Vinnie Jones, Dennis Wise and John Fashanu to work with a woman. But they loved her. She took no nonsense from any of them and they really respected her. She helped so many of them get back to fitness and she was always finding innovative ways to help them recover from injuries. Those players saw then what I would come to see much later on when I worked with her full time. She has a special aura about her. She can put her arm around you when you are down or if you have got problems at home. She gives you that confidence you need to keep pushing yourself.

Even though she was too busy to coach me, Jenny and I stayed in touch and she often used to ask me down to Wimbledon. The players always used to make me feel really welcome. Sometimes I went to games and sat in the dressing room while Vinnie and Dennis were running around doing their mad stuff before matches. One time when I was about twelve and Wimbledon played Crystal Palace at Selhurst Park I remember being allowed to sit in the dugout. That was brilliant. Even though I'm an Arsenal fan it was very special to be given the privilege to see this fantastic club up close.

In those days I was a shy boy and I just used to sit back

and take it all in. John Gayle was the player who probably looked out for me the most and who I got to know the best. He was a lovely man and was always giving me lifts or taking me out for dinner. He did so much for me.

All the members of the Crazy Gang were fantastic characters. What always struck me was that they seemed to enjoy playing so much. They loved every minute they were playing and while it was important to do your best, work your socks off and win, it was also important to have a laugh. That attitude really made a big impression on me and I have tried to follow the same principle in my sporting career. In those days Wimbledon never seemed to be under pressure. I am sure they were, but it never came across that way. They were a fantastic club and it is a real shame that there won't be another team like them – not in my lifetime anyway. The Premier League has changed beyond recognition from those early years when Wimbledon were a part of it. The gulf between a club like that and big teams like Arsenal and Manchester United was always huge – even back in the 1980s and early '90s. But in these days of super-rich foreign owners and multi-billion-pound TV deals it's hard to see how a little club that worked its way up from non-league football with attendances of just over 15,000 could ever hope to compete. It's a shame but football is now such a big business.

With Jenny busy at Wimbledon, I got my head down and started training at Tooting.

I loved those early days. It was such a buzz to do

something I really enjoyed. The sense of freedom was immense and it really helped to take the edge off those dark days when I would get upset about things. Whenever I felt like asking 'Why me?', I could now go out on the track and vent my anger. Maybe this is what gave me that desire, that hunger to try to do well and succeed in something.

My first coaches were a father-and-son duo called Chas and Dan Sadler. Chas was a very good wheelchair racer who often used to do the London Marathon and combined coaching down at the Tooting Bec track with a bit of racing. His son Dan, although able bodied, chose to race in a wheelchair. In those days there was nothing in the rules to prevent people without disabilities from racing in wheelchairs. It might seem a bit strange but because he grew up with his dad in a chair it was all very normal to him. Once in the chair he had no advantage over those in the same classification with disabilities and he raced the circuit for years.

But clearly not everyone understood why he was doing it. And a few years ago he hit the headlines when it emerged he had accepted prize money for competing in the Great North Run. Someone later spotted him getting out of his chair and told the papers and he had to hand the money back. It didn't bother me that he was able bodied but chose to race in a chair. The class was open to able-bodied people at the time anyway. I felt sorry for him when he got all this negative publicity because he was only doing a sport his dad was involved with and he was only doing it for fun. Maybe he shouldn't have taken the prize money but it probably wasn't very much.

Between them Chas and Dan came up with a training programme which instilled a bit of discipline into what I was doing. But even at that early age it was clear I had a bit of a gift. Sometimes I feel like I was put on this earth to race. I had naturally fast hand speed, I was light, and I had a good technique. I learned my own style and developed it very quickly. When I teach youngsters now, I obviously teach them the basics but I emphasise that they have to find and develop their own style that will work for them. You wouldn't expect Paula Radcliffe to run like Michael Johnson. There is a certain basic level of technique required for sprinting and long-distance running but they both have their own natural, distinctive style. It's just the same in wheelchair racing and it's something I don't believe you can teach.

Although some coaches I have worked with have tried to change my style, it's pretty much the same now as it was when I started. I generate the power from my shoulders. That's then passed down through the triceps, through the forearms, through the wrists into the push rims, which move my wheels. I also use a lot of my core strength, and the muscles in my chest. But it's not all about power. If it was then lighter athletes like my Swiss rival Marcel Hug would not be anywhere near the top. I could lift double the weights he can in the gym. But he's still got great speed in the chair.

It's all down to how your hands connect with the push rims. You need to be as efficient and fluent as possible. You want to be flowing and hit that push rim at the right time. You want a smooth rhythm and I try my best not to waste energy when I race. The jerkier you are the less efficient you are. You need to glide along the track. It's exactly like watching Mo Farah run, he seems to glide along on his toes. It doesn't look like he's expending any effort.

The pushing technique is not easy to master because you have to hit the wheel rims with such speed. It takes a lot of practice to master. As my arms move downward I half-clench my fists but leave my thumbs sticking out. My knuckles make contact with the push rim first, a fraction of a second before the thumb hits it, driving it down to the bottom of the push. I then flick off before lifting my arms and doing it all again. Some people might be more thumb, others are more knuckle. I am actually different on each hand – that's why if you study me closely you will see I use more thumb on my left hand than my right. It might be because my back is slightly crooked and so leads to me favouring one arm over the other. It's the tiniest of margins but when you are racing it can make a big difference.

Even from an early age I wanted to win everything, regardless of the distance. Whether it was 100m or 5,000m, I wanted to beat everyone. I don't think there was anyone else in my age group who could do the range of distances that I have always done. A lot of the strength came from walking around on callipers and I have always had big biceps and triceps and enormous hands. So I am thankful my mum and dad wanted me to walk around as a kid, instead of using a wheelchair. It made me much stronger. I didn't lift any weights until I was eighteen. I didn't know you had to. All my strength came through pushing my chair.

Maybe it was the strength but I always felt the training came easy – it was just a bit of fun. There were probably a few times when, as a teenager, I didn't want to go because I wanted to be out with my mates. But I didn't take it too seriously. I was just lucky I won so many races. By the time I was thirteen I was already racing with the Great Britain seniors. To race grown men and beat them was an amazing feeling. With Chas and Dan's guidance I got stronger and stronger and really started to develop as an athlete. And it was thanks to them that I got to my first Paralympics in Atlanta. They were a huge part of my early years.

Back in those days the chairs I raced in were nothing like the ones I have specially made for me now. My first one was paid for with a grant from Sutton Council. I immediately felt faster and loved it. I felt like a wheelchair racer. Although I have to admit it would look weird now up against the modern, streamlined machines we use today. It had four chunky wheels – three-wheelers were still quite a new thing back then. It looked a bit like a hospital trolley bed and it took a bit of getting used to.

We had a little path along the side of the house, so when I first got it I used to go up and down this path for hours on end. I really came to love it and I used it for quite a long time. It was made by a company called Bromakin, which was founded by the 1988 gold-medal-winning Paralympian Peter Carruthers. His is one of those amazing, inspiring stories that are so commonplace in disability sport.

He was working as a plumber when he was badly injured in a car crash and left needing to use a wheelchair. His desire to race and compete led him to adapt his own chair and to develop a whole range of modern racing machines. I wish I still had that first chair but I think I left it at the track for someone else to use. When you are younger you don't value old things, you always want the latest bit of kit on the market. For me it was a bit like moving on to a new car. I never looked back.

With Chas and Dan overseeing my training I gradually increased the number of races I took part in. They were all over the country and my parents used to give up so much of their time and money to make sure I could compete. At first it was my mum who used to ferry me around all over the place because my dad hadn't passed his driving test. Then he got his licence and for the next six or seven years he gave up much of his life to help me compete and train. He used to leave home for work at 6 a.m., come back twelve hours later and then take me out to training. He would never eat, he would just take me straight to Tooting Bec. It was an amazing sacrifice, day after day. Then he was forking out for all the races around the country. I was extremely fortunate that my mum and dad had two full-time jobs so we were OK, but they were hardly rolling in it and paying for their son's racing ambitions must have caused quite a hefty dent in the family bank account. Apart from the grant for the chair there were no sponsors or charities to pay for the petrol or the entry fees.

But my parents just wanted me to do well and saw that it was giving their son a focus and a sense of normality. So for my old man, if that meant loading up the red Ford Escort and heading off on the motorway for hours on end then so be it. There were so many race meetings back when I was a junior. And it was surprisingly competitive, with athletes in a whole range of classes. Nowadays when you go to them you are lucky to get a couple of athletes in each class. But Stoke Mandeville was always my favourite. I started going there from the age of nine or ten. It was here that the Paralympic movement started and where the first Games, inspired by Professor Sir Ludwig Guttmann, were held back in 1948. Everywhere you look there's a reminder of the place's heritage. You can't help but be moved and inspired. It just has an aura about it, a sense of history, and anyone who goes there immediately understands its significance. During training camps it was a who's who of Paralympic sport. But the person who always made me feel most at ease was also the most successful wheelchair athlete of her generation. Tanni Grey-Thompson was one of my earliest heroines and to meet her as a young athlete starting out was such a privilege. Because she is so down to earth and approachable it's easy to forget she has achieved so much as an athlete, but from the very first day we met at Stoke Mandeville she always backed me. She would watch how I trained and give me little tips and she was always checking I was OK. To have people like Tanni telling you that you had great talent gave the newcomers like me great confidence. It really helped keep me motivated. In those days there wasn't a nice hotel where athletes could stay – we were all accommodated in giant dormitories where twenty or thirty people could sleep. Despite that I always liked going – even though the track in those early days was bumpy. You didn't get looked at as odd or different. It was the British home of Paralympic sport. Rubbing shoulders with the best in the country from other sports such as basketball, swimming, archery, table tennis and shooting made you feel part of a very exclusive club. To me it felt like home. And it reaffirmed that this was where I wanted to be. At that stage the only event that mattered to me was the London Marathon. I became slightly obsessed by it. By the time I was thirteen I had mastered the mini version, winning it comfortably. Now I wanted to test myself with the full distance. That was always my dream, my FA Cup Final at Wembley. At least, it was until the summer of 1992. That's when I got the Paralympic bug.

Barcelona – blue skies and sunshine, divers leaping off the high board framed by Gaudí's Sagrada Família, Sally Gunnell winning gold for Great Britain and that archer lighting the sacred flame. That summer's Olympics was one of the most memorable for years. But it wasn't those Games which captured my imagination. It was what followed a couple of weeks later that turned my world upside down.

And the athlete who got me hooked? A Swiss wheelchair racer called Heinz Frei. He ruled the Paralympics that year and won the marathon in front of a crowd of 65,000 people in the Olympic Stadium. He was a phenomenal athlete who dominated races. I remember watching all this on the BBC as a thirteen-year-old and thinking, 'I want to be him.' I kept a lot of this to myself, though. In those days I was very awkward and shy. When I wasn't with my friends or really close family I could feel extremely self-conscious and didn't really like talking to people. It was the same sort of feelings all teenagers have, but when you are in a wheelchair you feel even more uncomfortable expressing your ideas and ambitions. But my eyes were popping out of my head whenever I watched Heinz race in Barcelona. His performances had a very deep impact on me. He's well into his fifties now but during his career he won fourteen Paralympic gold medals in summer and winter Games. That is the amazing thing about him: he won gold in cross-country skiing as well as wheelchair athletics. And he's still racing now. In fact, I have to admit that he came quite close to beating me in the 2013 London Marathon.

It was hardly a surprise that with all this going on my studies at school had taken a back seat. Suddenly, the only thing that mattered was getting to the Atlanta Games in four years' time. By the time I took my GCSEs in 1994 I had already decided to focus on my sport. That partly explains my poor results: all E and F grades. Complete rubbish. I blamed the school a little bit: the English coursework was given to us too late and there were other lessons I wanted to do which weren't available to me. In the end, PE was my best grade (hardly a shock). But it wasn't all down to the school. I should have studied more.

But at that time I simply couldn't wait to get away. So I tried studying at a couple of colleges – first, tourism at a place called Nescot, just outside Epsom in Surrey. I found it dull and, irritatingly, a load of the same kids I had grown up with at Bedelsford followed me there. My heart sank when I turned up and saw a lot of the old faces. I wanted to escape the confines of a school which reminded me of my physical limitations. I know now, looking back, that it might seem a bit childish but at that stage I didn't want to be held back any more. In the end, all I really learned was how to play pool in the college bar. Tourism wasn't for me. I was summoned to see the head of the college.

'What are you playing at?' he asked me. 'Why don't you get your head down and work for a qualification? Don't you want to make something of yourself?'

But my heart wasn't in it. So I told him I didn't want to do this any more. There and then, I quit. As I wheeled myself out of his office I remember feeling liberated but scared. I had a knot in my stomach and my mouth was dry. I knew I had made the right decision but I had no idea what I was going to do next.

Music has always been a big part of my life. I love house music and fancy myself as a bit of a DJ. So when the chance came up to study music at another local college in

Carshalton, I thought it might be the answer. Unlike tourism, this felt more up my street. But that didn't work either. I wasn't made to be in classrooms and, although I knew I was bright enough to learn, my confidence and self-esteem were rock bottom. I would panic whenever it was my turn to speak in a class, the nerves made me sick. I was embarrassed at my inability to read and spell properly. So once again I quit education, this time for good. I felt completely betrayed, angry and lost. Sport would have to be my escape.

CHAPTER 4

FOOL'S GOLD

The Barcelona Paralympics was a turning point in my life. Those golden images of my new heroes Heinz Frei and Tanni Grey-Thompson winning in front of huge, excited crowds convinced me that this was my future. Representing my country at a Paralympics now became my mission, the 1996 Games in Atlanta my dream.

For the three years after that I worked so hard to become a better athlete, developing my technique, building my strength and fitness and learning the tactical skills that you need to win races. In those days I was a pure sprinter. I was still too young to have worked out what I wanted to specialise in, although even back then I preferred the middle-distance events – the 800m and 1,500m.

The truth is, sprinting is really boring. The training is repetitive and I just don't enjoy it. Tactically, the middle-distance races are far more challenging, while in the 100m, if you don't get the start right then the race is over. And if you suffer from nerves, like me, then getting off to a good start is extremely difficult. I was always so worried about false starting that I couldn't relax. In training, I could break the world record, no problem. But when it came to race day, I would freeze. Consistency was my big problem. Some days I could nail the start and move through all the various phases of the race without a single mistake. Other times it would go pear shaped from the off. If I can get myself in contention with 30 or 40 metres to go then I know I have the top-end speed to win. But often I left myself way too much to do.

Despite all those concerns the sprint events offered me my best chance of getting to Atlanta. Competition for the middle-distance events was fierce – they attracted the best athletes – and I knew I was a promising sprinter. So for now I focused on the 100m, 200m and 400m. As far as I was concerned I just wanted to represent my country, go to the Games and do my best. If the shorter distances got me my golden ticket to the Games, then so what?

As Atlanta drew ever nearer I knew I was in contention. But it was a major battle to get the qualifying times I needed to get picked by the GB selectors. So, in the early part of 1996 I was a young man on a mission. I spent weeks chasing around the country trying to get the standard. In the end I only made the qualifying time by the skin of my teeth – about a day short of the cut-off point in May. I knew I was improving all the time and that the selectors might be looking to blood some new talent. The team wasn't that strong and there were only a couple of real gold-medal contenders – Tanni Grey-Thompson and Dave Holding, a four-time winner of the London Marathon who didn't win a medal in Barcelona but was favourite to win gold over 100m in Atlanta. Apart from those two, the team was in transition. I knew I had a good chance.

But would the selectors take a chance on me? I knew I could beat a lot of the older guys in the British team over lots of different distances but I was still racked with self-doubt, just praying to get my chance.

Then I got the phone call. It was a moment I will never forget. I felt so proud. It was such an honour, such a privilege. It was out of this world. There were huge cheers when I told my mum, dad and brothers. Remember, this was a huge moment for my family, who had given so much to help me reach this point. I just kept thinking how special it would be for a boy to come from a south London council estate and represent his country at the Paralympics. We were overjoyed. My brothers had boxed to a really good standard ... but to represent your country? That was another level. They really understood what it meant and were so proud. Then there were my coaches – Chas and Dan Sadler and, of course, Jenny. Everyone had worked so hard to get me to Atlanta and now it was actually going to happen. I was so excited.

Because there were twelve days between the Olympics ending and the Paralympics starting I remember watching events unfold in America with an anticipation I had never experienced before. We had to leave just before the closing ceremony, but those highlights still made a big impression on me. Muhammad Ali lighting the cauldron and Michael Johnson smashing the world record in the 200m – these were some of the unforgettable moments in sporting history and I was going to be a small part of it.

But it was also an Olympics cursed by a nail bomb attack in an Atlanta park which killed one person and wounded more than 100 others. And it was a Games marred by transport and organisational headaches. There had been lots of reports of athletes getting lost on buses and missing their events, and of the food being awful. But at that stage it didn't bother me. I just tried to put all that out of my mind and focus on my racing.

I remember the excitement building as I went to collect my GB kit at a special camp set up by the British Paralympic Association in Birmingham. Just meeting the other members of the team was a fantastic feeling. Then, before I knew it, I was on my way to Gatwick Airport to join the team and fly to America. My mum dropped me off. She was in floods of tears, but I wasn't scared. I was happy to go away and to be in another country, to see the other side of the world. I wasn't even worried about the flight – which was extraordinary because I am now so terrified of flying that I drive to most of my race meetings in Europe. Back then I wasn't afraid, though – it's only something that's developed as I got older. In fact, the plane to Atlanta had a problem and we were all sat on the tarmac for ages waiting for the engineers to fix it. If that happened now I would be straight out the door. But for me, getting to compete in the Paralympics was so important that a wing would have had to fall off to stop me getting on the plane.

When we eventually landed in Atlanta we got straight onto a bus and were taken to the British team's training camp at the US Naval Air Station, Pensacola. Situated about five hours' drive south-west of Atlanta on the Gulf of Mexico, it was a great place to prepare for the Games. The facilities were first rate but it was also nice and quiet. We didn't have any distractions or disturbances. And, of course, it was totally secure. To be there training every day with the top athletes in Britain made me feel really special.

After we arrived everyone was so jet-lagged. This was my first real taste of big international competition and although I had been to Australia as a junior, this was a big step up. Sadly there was no one else of a similar age in the team that I could talk to. Instead I relied on the older, more experienced athletes like Dave Holding – my roommate – and Tanni. She looked after me quite a lot. She would always make sure I was presentable in my GB kit and said if I needed any help to just come and ask her.

Our two weeks at Pensacola flashed by. Soon it was time to head up to Atlanta. My bags packed, I sat in my day chair outside the apartment blocks, waiting to board the coach for the biggest adventure of my life. The heat was unbearable: 35 degrees in the shade. And the humidity – just breathing made you sweat. After a few minutes waiting, my shiny new GB kit was soaked. It was like I had been caught in a sudden shower. I wondered to myself, 'How on earth am I going to race in this?' Climbing onto the ice-cold, air-conditioned coach was such a relief. Now I felt shivery as I took my seat next to Dave. He checked if I was OK. I was fine. Shitting a brick with nerves, but basically OK.

As the bus pulled onto the highway I sat silently, staring out of the window at America's wide open spaces. The giant juggernauts with their shiny chrome radiators, so distinctive and different to what we are used to back in England. The scale of everything, the width of the highways. It was awesome. Exciting.

For the first couple of weeks in America, everything was fine. It was only when we got to the athletes' village that people started to ask questions. Was this really how an Olympic and Paralympic village was supposed to be? The accommodation was situated on a university campus, so it hadn't been specially built for the Games. But the rooms were so small. Everyone got an apartment shared between four or six people but the bedrooms and bathrooms were shared. The twin bedrooms were so tiny that by the time you got a wardrobe in there and a bedside table, there was only enough space for one wheelchair between the beds. For athletes like me this was such a terrible oversight. Only one of us could have our chair in the bedroom area at once. How were we both supposed to get into bed?

It was lucky I was sharing with Dave. He was an old hand at big events and had learned to take things as they come. Plus he didn't snore. He was so quiet that I had to keep checking if he was still there. In the end we worked out a pretty good system so we could both manoeuvre ourselves into bed. I would wheel myself into the tiny room first. Then he got as close to the door as he could and would swing himself across the bed and under his covers. His chair would stay by the door while mine sat between the two beds. If I had rolled over I would have ended up falling into it. It was a disgrace. How on earth could the organisers say these rooms had been adapted for people like me?

But this was just the beginning. Getting to the food hall was a nightmare. There were big, steep hills across the campus so just getting from your apartment to breakfast or lunch was really hard work in a wheelchair. Fortunately we were all fit enough to cope with it but on the race days we didn't really want to be wasting energy just going to get a bite to eat. So some of the wheelchair athletes would hitch a lift on the back of the little trains the organisers were running to get people around the site. It was hilarious.

But once you got to the food hall you didn't feel like laughing. It was ridiculous. It was so small – a tiny fraction of the size of the one we had in London. You had to queue for over an hour just to get a bit of breakfast. And then there were flies everywhere. It was disgusting. I don't know if it was the same for the Olympic guys a few weeks earlier but I guess it must have been. It was supposed to be a first-class experience designed for the best athletes in the world – but it didn't feel that way. Most of it wasn't made for us and it was clear Atlanta didn't really think of the Paralympians. Fortunately, I never got caught out on the buses – my drivers always seemed to know where they were going. Maybe by the time the Paralympics came around they had learned the various routes. But I do remember going to the warm-up area, which was in the middle of quite a rough and dangerous part of town. At the time I didn't even think about it – all I cared about was racing. But when you look back you think, 'Blimey, that could have been deadly.'

The most shattering disappointment of Atlanta was the crowds. Hardly anyone came out to see us. Those who did sit in the stands were mostly volunteers or staff from the Atlanta organising committee. I felt so let down. They would probably tell you differently but to me it looked like very few people had actually paid to come and watch us. For the 100m final the stadium was completely empty. I don't know if the International Paralympic Committee or the American organisers were to blame. I have very little respect for the IPC – the same thing happened to us at the World Championships in New Zealand (more of which later). They just didn't seem to promote it. I am convinced that if Atlanta had been promoted properly then people would have come and watched. But we were an after-thought. The Paralympics is supposed to be parallel to the Olympics but we didn't feel parallel to anything. It felt like – and I hate this word – the 'special' Games. Back in the UK there was hardly any interest either. There were highlights on the BBC but the newspapers barely gave it a mention. It was very upsetting.

As for the British team – it was all done on a bit of a shoestring. Not like now, with hundreds of millions of pounds provided by the National Lottery. There was no backroom team of note. We had physios and medical staff, but there was no coach giving us tactics or sports psychologist giving advice going into a race. The British Paralympic Association even had to buy its own kit from Adidas. Some of it was made for us but the vast majority was the same as the Olympic team. Except that the 'British Olympics 1996 Atlanta' badge had been replaced by a clunky Paralympics one sewn over the top. It was real budget stuff. I actually ended up taking the Paralympic logo off mine because I thought the Olympic one was better. The kit was very patched up. Despite that, it's the one kit I have kept: it has such sentimental value for me. I've even got the marching kit from the opening ceremony. It was all very classic British, made by Aquascutum – navy blue and a yellow tie. The opening ceremony was an impressive affair – and at least the stadium was sold out for that. I remember the *Superman* actor Christopher Reeve hosting it. Only a year earlier he had been paralysed in a horse-riding accident, so it took incredible bravery to do what he did. It was a very moving moment for everyone. But perhaps we should have seen what was coming when it was left to US Vice-President Al Gore – instead of the President, Bill Clinton – to open the Paralympics. Clinton didn't miss the Olympics, did he?

Despite all these distractions and disappointments, I had come all this way for one thing: the racing. And once at the track I just focused on my preparations. For a rookie like me it was just amazing to suddenly be alongside the very best. Athletes like the Canadian racer Jeff Adams, and the man who had inspired me four years earlier in Spain, Heinz Frei.

Jeff was the top dog. Some people thought he was a bit cocky but I thought he was a real character. Sure, he could come over as a bit full of himself but he was always nice to me. He could be very aggressive on the track but he always had respect for me. The great thing about Atlanta was that there was no pressure on me to deliver. It was my first Games and no one expected me to come home with medals of any colour. Tanni had been giving me a lot of advice in the run-up to my first heat. She had told me to keep calm and just go out and enjoy it.

So that was exactly what I did. In the 100m I got through my heat and then squeezed through the semi-final by a few hundredths of a second. I had a big smile from then on – my first Paralympics and my first final. I didn't care what I did after that.

The day of the final was another Atlanta scorcher. It was like a furnace out there. I thought the track might melt it was so hot. Still, hot weather made for fast times and this was a straight contest between my roommate Dave and the Swede Håkan Ericsson. They had been battling it out with each other all season, breaking world records and competing for gold. On the night it was Dave's race. He gave an awesome performance, smashed the world record and won the gold. I finished seventh and was so pleased. All I wanted to do was avoid coming last. It seems so unambitious now, but that was my big target then.

I knew I had less of a chance in my other event, the 400m. I would have to set personal bests to get through to the final. I got through the first round but was eliminated in the semi-finals – but only by two hundredths of a second. I had produced personal bests in both races, but they weren't good enough. It was a real sign of just how much better I would have to be to progress in the more competitive races.

I was pleased with how I performed in Atlanta. After all, it was my first Paralympics and I didn't expect to win gold medals. But while I thought I could shut out all the external stuff – the poor crowds, the bad organisation, the lack of interest back home – I couldn't. I came away feeling desperately disappointed. I had really put the Games on a pedestal and they had let me down in a big way. When I got back to London I thought, 'Why have I wasted my teenage years doing this?'

Atlanta showed me that people didn't give a stuff about Paralympic sport. I had got on that plane to Atlanta expecting the wow factor. Instead it just felt like a sideshow, with disabled athletes being paraded around like animals. When I look back on Atlanta now I can only wonder what Games prior to that must have been like. Was Seoul even worse? I had just assumed that because the Games were in North

America they would be blinding. I thought the Americans would want to be the best. But they just didn't seem to plan properly for them.

After Atlanta I did try to keep training and racing. But a lot of my motivation had been destroyed by my experience in the States. I was struggling to keep my place in the British team so, in December, four months after the Atlanta Games I had worked so hard to get to, I just thought, that's it. I quit. There's nothing in it for me any more.

My parents couldn't understand what I was doing. They thought I had so much to be proud of and said it would get better in the future. That was all that anyone said. But I just didn't feel that way. I had started too young. Got addicted to it too young. Not because of my parents pushing me: they never got involved with the training and never made me do anything I didn't want to do. All they did was take me to the races and back me up. They did everything I asked of them.

The fact was, my outlook on life was changing. I was seventeen and yet I had spent all my teenage years training and keeping fit. Everything I did was aimed at one day representing my country at the Paralympics. Well, now I had done it, and it wasn't what I thought it was going to be. All my mates were suddenly going out drinking and having a laugh and I just wanted a part of that. I felt left out.

On top of all this I had been involved in a relationship with a girl called Maxine whom I had started seeing before Atlanta. We had been together a while – my first serious relationship. I met her at a youth club. She had made the first move. At that stage of my life I never chatted up girls. I was too scared. I waited until they approached me. I wasn't worried about my looks; I was pretty sure girls fancied me. But I always worried that they couldn't see past the chair. After a few rejections and knock-backs I retreated inside myself. I asked myself, why would anyone want to go out with me? A bloke in a wheelchair? I was full of self-doubt and although it really got on my nerves, there wasn't too much I could do to overcome it back then. So, to be in a relationship gave me a great sense of security. Imagine my horror when I got back home from America to find out she had started seeing other blokes while I was away. I was only young but it deeply affected me and I got a bit depressed. I asked myself, 'Is it my disability? Is this why she's done this? Is this why I can't get a proper girlfriend?'

At that point I couldn't see a way through it all. My sport was supposed to be my escape from my disability – a way of turning my misfortune into something unique and special. But Atlanta had let me down. I was lost.

———

This was always going to be the hardest bit to write. As I sit here now, preparing to bare my soul, to confess my past sins, I'm finding it hard to breathe. Even saying the words aloud to the empty room is difficult. I go to open my mouth and start speaking but I feel blood rush to my face. I'm full of self-loathing and shame. Did it really happen? Was it really that bad? After all, everyone's at it, aren't they?

But I know deep down there's no excuse. I should have known better. What a waste. What an idiot.

Normally I am so controlled but my anxiety is overwhelming. I take a sip of water and tell myself to get on with it. I imagine it's like a really tough training session that I just have to get through. At the end I will be better for it, but right now it feels like the world is going to end.

When I decided to write this book, I weighed up the pros and cons of coming clean on what really happened to me when I quit the sport after the Atlanta Games. For years I have kept it a closely guarded secret. Only my family, Jenny and my closest friends know what really went on. Even my dad doesn't know the truth.

Those who know me will understand. They may not even be that surprised.

But those who don't know me may jump to conclusions. I only hope that when people read my story they will understand that I was in a dark place. It was over ten years ago and I have learned from my mistakes.

Ultimately, the public will have to make their own minds up but I can only do what I feel to be right and right now I want to get this off my chest. I have been carrying it around for too long.

It all started when I was out at a party with some of my closest mates. Frustrated and bored, I was going out a lot. My mum and dad said I treated their house like a hotel.

With no job and no prospect of finding one, house music became my new escape. It was 1997 and although Blur and Oasis were still keeping the Britpop scene going, I was only interested in dance music. I used to go to a lot of clubs and raves in those days – Vauxhall, Camden, anywhere in London, really. Drugs were everywhere. A lot of my older mates had started getting involved a few years earlier. It was just a part of the social scene back then.

Going down the pub? Take drugs.

Going clubbing? Take drugs.

Going to a rave? Get completely out of your head.

The weird thing is I had always shunned it. In fact, I hated it. As far as I was concerned it was fine for my mates to mess about. It was their life and they could do what they liked. But, crucially, I didn't envy them or want to join in. I had my training and my Paralympic ambitions. Why would I get caught up in all that?

Besides, I was absolutely terrified of dying. I hated the idea that I would take something and then collapse or have a fit. I'd read all the scare stories about kids overheating and dying from taking pills and I didn't want to end up like that.

For a sportsman, too, the potential repercussions are enormous. OK, so this was different – purely recreational stuff. But drugs of any sort carry such a stigma for athletes. I don't want anyone to think that what I am about to confess in any way changes my attitude towards performance-enhancing drugs in sport. So, let me be clear. I do not condone the use of any banned substances to cheat. Those who take steroids or EPO or whatever to get an advantage are undermining our sport and are ruining it for the rest. That's why I am always happy when I see people being caught. They deserve to be punished. The longer the ban, the better. But after the heart-breaking experience of Atlanta, all my boundaries went. I no longer had a reason to say no, a higher objective which required me to lead a clean, healthy lifestyle. I had always wanted to be one of the gang, to fit in. Now I could be. So, when my mates offered me drugs I started to get curious. I was tempted.

I would like to say I remember exactly where I was and who I was with when I first tried it, but I can't. Maybe it was the effects of what I took or perhaps, and this is far more likely, it's a self-defence mechanism, my embarrassment forcing me to erase the detail. All I know is that it was at a party and that one of my mates offered me some recreational drugs. At first I refused, I think, but then I gave in. It didn't really seem to do anything. Maybe I was a bit more energetic. Maybe the music sounded a bit better. But was this it? It hardly seemed to be worth all the fuss.

But after that first little experiment my inhibitions fell away. I had taken drugs and lived to tell the tale. It wasn't anywhere near as scary as I thought it was going to be. I was still taking my first tentative steps into the world of drugs and while I was definitely getting braver all the time, I didn't shed all my fears overnight.

For a while I kept it under control. It was just a thing I

did at weekends. I looked forward to the buzz of getting high. Meeting up with my mates, being one of the gang. The music was great and I was loving the sense of freedom and normality. When you are off your face, no one gives a shit if you are in a wheelchair. In fact it came with a few advantages. For example, I never had to queue to get into clubs – the bouncers always waved me through. And they never, ever searched me, while everyone else was given the cursory frisking and asked to turn out their pockets.

But things quickly got out of hand. As the months went on my barriers got lower and lower and the number of times I took drugs grew higher and higher. Suddenly I was taking a lot of drugs. I never strayed into the really hard stuff. My group of friends weren't into that sort of stuff. We might have been stupid but we weren't completely insane.

But looking back over this period I guess I must have been addicted in a mild way. Whether it was the escape I craved or the music, somehow it all came to be associated with getting out of it. I even started smoking cigarettes. I often ask myself, 'How come I didn't do myself some long-term damage?' I guess the answer is luck. And money.

If I had been rolling in it then I could have developed a major problem. As it was I spent nearly all my spare cash on drink, drugs and going out. It was all right for my mates – they all had jobs and had a bit of spare cash. But here I was, a disabled bloke, no job and on benefits. I borrowed loads of money from my mum and dad and then just spent it on drugs.

Not all my mates were comfortable with what I was doing. They would ask me, 'What are you doing, Dave? What about your racing?'

They tried to get me to see sense and stop. Although they were the ones who got me into the stuff, they never forced me to do it. It was always my choice.

My parents must have known something was going on – I used to creep back into the house after a big night out, go upstairs, have a shower and then go straight back out again so they didn't spot me. But when you are a parent you only see what you want to see. And I was very secretive. I never did anything in front of people they knew, anyone who might have allowed them to get an idea. My dad was already upset that I had turned my back on sport. He had invested so much time and money supporting me and now I was just wasting it all. He must have been heartbroken.

As for my brothers, Alan knew and he didn't like it one little bit. At one point he really lost it with me. But what could he do? He could only tell me. He couldn't hold my hand for twenty-four hours a day. He would say, 'You know this won't last.' 'It's just a phase,' he would say.

I was a smart arse back then, though: 'Well, if it's just a phase, then I'll be OK, won't I? Look, Alan, I just don't want to go back to racing. I am done with it.'

'Then you're wasting your life, aren't you?'

It just washed over me.

It was now two years on from Atlanta and I should have been fine-tuning my preparations to represent Great

Britain at the 1998 World Championships on home soil in Birmingham. Instead I was spending most of my time in nightclubs like the Colosseum in Vauxhall or the Camden Palace.

It was a very, very bad time. And after having started so cautiously, now I wasn't sure if I could stop. The next day I would feel like shit. You would ask yourself why you were doing it all just for a night out. My answer? Go out the following weekend and do it all over again.

So what changed? How did I turn my life around?

It just stopped being fun. After almost three years of hammering my brain with drugs, I was starting to get paranoid. I'll never forget the moment I saw one bloke in Camden really freaking out. He had taken too much of something and was panicking. He thought people were trying to get him. That scared me. Why wasn't that happening to me?

A little while after that I was watching TV with a mate after a heavy night out. I was too wired to go to bed and needed something to help me get to sleep. Suddenly he started fitting. I can remember it so vividly. He was so scared he was shaking. I held him and told him he would be fine and that whatever it was he was experiencing would pass. Eventually it did pass. But it had really sobered me up. We both knew it had been quite serious. And for me, that was way too close to home. I had to stop.

At that point I got a lucky break. I met Kaylie.

For the last few years I hadn't been interested in girls or

getting involved in a relationship. I was having too much fun to get tied down. But Kaylie came along at exactly the right moment. I was attracted to her. She was a bit younger than me and my friends but she was quite streetwise. She knew what my mates and I were into. She liked a drink herself but she wasn't into taking drugs or anything like that. I don't know why but Kaylie wanted to help me get out of the mess I had made for myself. She knew I needed saving and she asked me the question the drugs had been blocking out for so long: 'Dave, what exactly do you want to do in your life?'

I had no answer. I wanted to work but I had lost all my confidence in the system. What employer was going to give me a chance? Who would look past the wheelchair? I wasn't clever enough to study and, besides, I had tried that and couldn't stand it. I needed money but my benefits gave me more than I would probably earn. What was the point? Wheelchair racing was the only thing I was any good at, I told her.

'So why don't you go back to it?' she said.

———

It sounded so simple. But I knew I had upset a lot of people. I had just vanished off the scene. I had missed the World Championships and I knew UK Athletics and my coaches were upset with me. I had been on another planet. I had let a lot of people down. No one really tried to find me while I was out of the sport. My mum had a few phone calls from people in the sport but I wasn't interested. It must have been so upsetting for my parents because they knew that I could have had a good career.

The road back would be long and painful. I returned to training slowly, seeking out my old coaches, Chas and Dan. They said they were prepared to pick up where we left off but that there would be some new ground rules. 'We don't know what you have been up to,' they told me. 'And frankly we don't care. But if you are coming training, we are here at this time on these days. Don't let us down.'

So I had to prove a point. At first, it was hard. Even doing a few laps was difficult. I had put on a fair bit of weight and was wheezing from smoking fags for three years. I was in terrible shape. But I kept at it. I went to training three times a week, just for something else to do. Something to keep me from falling back into bad habits. A combination of Kaylie's encouragement, the training and my sheer stubbornness helped me get through it. After a while – maybe three months – I felt like I had turned a corner. In the back of my mind I was a bit worried about what might happen if I really pushed my body. After all the punishment it had taken, how might it react? Would it trigger something really nasty – either mental or physical? And how long does this shit stay in your system? What if I want to race competitively again and get drug tested? Will it always be there?

At first, I didn't want to think about racing and competing again. Dan was going to the Sydney Paralympics in the autumn of 2000 and although I was really excited for him, I didn't think it was going to bother me too much.

But when I saw it on TV I broke down. I couldn't stop crying. I kept asking myself, 'What have I done?'

Seeing those golden images from Australia – Tanni and all the other British athletes winning medals, the crowds, the atmosphere. It just killed me. I couldn't help but feel that I had tossed away four years of my life. And on what?

Absolutely nothing. I couldn't even remember most of it. It was just so sad. I cried for hours and hours.

Even now, I still feel that sense of regret. Things have turned out OK but I am still deeply ashamed and embarrassed by what I did. I wish it hadn't happened and I hate to think how my kids and other members of my family who didn't know all this will react when they read this and see how stupid I was. As a parent now, I would hate my three children to go anywhere near drugs. If there is one good thing to come out of the experience it is that I totally understand the damage people can do themselves. I was lucky: I don't seem to have done myself any harm. Equally, people shouldn't get the wrong impression about what went on. I wasn't some kind of junkie. I wasn't. It was a terrible phase of my life, but it was part of growing up. Rebelling. And, ultimately – like it or not – it is part of my story.

And how do I feel now that I have got it off my chest?

Lighter. Like a load has been lifted from my shoulders. It was such a long time ago and there is something comforting in knowing you have been through something like that and survived. In fact, I know it made me stronger, helped shape my character.

The Sydney Games was the wake-up call I needed. Even though I had started training again it wasn't until the Games started that it really hit home. I had let so many people down: my family, my coaches and myself. I had let my sport down. Now, I finally knew that this was what I wanted. As long as I could race I would never miss a Paralympics again.

CHAPTER 5

A SECOND CHANCE

Watching the Sydney Olympics and Paralympics in the autumn of 2000 was a devastating experience. For the rest of the nation, getting up early to see Sir Steve Redgrave winning his fifth Olympic gold medal or Tanni Grey-Thompson winning her fourth in the Paralympics must have been a joyous celebration. The Olympics had set a new gold standard – but it was the way the Australians embraced the Paralympics that really changed the game.

The organisers sold a record 1.2 million tickets and for the first time it felt like the Paralympics was being treated seriously. Compared to Atlanta, this was another world. After the Olympics closing ceremony Australians just couldn't accept that the party was over. They threw themselves just as enthusiastically into the Paralympics. There were sell-out crowds, the media gave it big coverage and, for the first time, thanks in part to the introduction of National Lottery funding a few years earlier, there was a real turnaround in British fortunes. The Australian team stole the show but, for me, Tanni produced the outstanding performance of the Games, winning the 100m, 200m, 400m and 800m. Her achievements in Sydney were a real inspiration to me.

These were exciting times for British sport and yet I was currently playing no part in it. Seeing Tanni do so well was amazing but it left me feeling distraught. I have always loved competing for my country – maybe it's my dad's army upbringing or growing up on a working-class council estate. You are just taught to love being English and British. I feel so passionate about pulling on the GB vest and doing battle for my country. I knew I owed my country some medals.

I had packed in taking drugs long before Sydney. Kaylie had helped me see sense. I was back training again with Chas and Dan Sadler and, while it was tough and my body was in a mess, it felt good to have a focus again. But at that point I thought representing my country again was just a pipe dream. The training was just a distraction – something to keep my mind off all the other rubbish. While I dearly wanted a second chance and to line up at the Athens Paralympics in 2004, deep down I didn't really believe I could come back.

But at least I now had a routine in my life. I was training three days a week and getting back into the swing of things. At home, things were a bit more settled. I was twenty-one now and had been with Kaylie for about a year. It was my first real relationship and back then she was my saviour.

She really helped get my head straight. I was now totally focused on racing again.

To be honest, I didn't have too many alternatives. Every time I went to the job centre it was a pretty depressing experience. I didn't want an office job. That wasn't me. I couldn't contemplate sitting behind a desk doing basic filing and answering the phone. It would have driven me mad. From time to time, more practical jobs would come up. Those were much more interesting. I went for one job at a small electronics company a couple of miles away. It involved soldering parts, so I went along for an interview and did the little test every candidate was asked to do. I am pretty sure I passed but in the end the job was given to someone else, someone with more experience. And yet on the application form it specifically said you didn't need experience. I felt so dejected I told the job centre I was no longer interested in finding work. I was done. Whenever I was sat in a waiting room for an interview and someone able bodied came in, I knew that was it. Before I had even said a word. It was a waste of time. I got fed up with being judged as stupid. No one was looking at me as a person, they just saw my chair.

These days it's very different. It's changed dramatically. If I was in that situation now, having to go for those same jobs, I would feel far more comfortable, like I had a genuine chance. Of course, some companies do it because they feel they have to; it's just a token gesture. A lot of people would resent that or see it as patronising. I don't. It doesn't bother me in the slightest. I am not going to quibble with anything which gives disabled people a chance of earning money and having a career. As far as I am concerned, it's great.

But racing was my only option back then. It was the only thing that offered me a chance of making something of my life and earning some money, even if it wasn't very much. The first priority was to get myself back into shape. In that first year or so I didn't do a lot of racing. I needed to get up to speed. Surprisingly, the body wasn't too bad. But I would have loads of mood swings and get very low and tired. I still get them now when I train too much. That's why I always go off and train in the morning, then come back in the afternoon. Then the kids can scream all they like, it just washes over me. In one ear and out the other. But the mood swings I get now are nothing compared to the downs I would get then. I guess it was something to do with the drugs.

After a while, training without racing lost its attraction. Things were going all right with Chas and Dan but it had been two years since I had come back and now I needed to step up a gear. I needed a kick up the arse. So I called Jenny.

I knew her number off by heart – I had been ringing it since I was ten. She knew my voice straight away. I told her I needed some help. At first she was worried about how Chas and Dan would react. But I explained that Chas was getting on a bit and that Dan had decided to go off and join the police. They were fine about it and had even encouraged me to get back in touch with her. I went down and met her on a Monday night down at the track. We talked about how I wanted to be part of the Great Britain team again. How I wanted to get to Athens.

'Do you think it's realistic?' I asked her.

'Yes. I'll get you there, Dave.'

But it was going to hurt. Jenny nearly killed me. She made me work so hard. I realised that all this time I had been coasting. There were times when I used to say to Chas or Dan, I don't fancy this drill or that drill or I'm not really in the mood today. Jenny made it clear from the very beginning that she wouldn't accept anything like that. If I wasn't prepared to do what she told me, it was over. Finished, there and then. I needed that boot up the arse; I needed to be pushed.

Within a month I noticed the difference. My speed was picking up and my body was getting stronger all the time. In the early part of 2002 I joined up with some of the other British athletes on a warm-weather training trip in Malaga. It went really well and as I approached the London Marathon – my first big race since I had turned my back on the sport – I knew I was in really good shape.

From the moment I first got hooked on wheelchair racing as a kid, winning the London Marathon had been my big ambition. It was the race I grew up watching and dreaming about. The one race I always watched which showed that disabled athletes could compete alongside those who were able bodied.

Lining up for the start, I felt an overwhelming sense of

pride and excitement. I couldn't believe I was here after everything I had been through. Now I had to prove to Jenny, my family and myself that I could win.

I got a bit of luck along the way. About 14 or 15 miles into the race the leader, a French guy called Pierre Fairbank, had a nasty crash, colliding head on with a traffic island in the middle of the road. Thankfully, he was OK, but I came past him, hit the front and never looked back. I might have caught him anyway, but I wasn't going to worry about how I won my first marathon, I was just going to make the most of the opportunity. All I could remember was Jenny telling me that if you hit the front, don't look behind you. Just keep going. So that's what I did. For ten miles I just drove on. It was a fantastic feeling. It was the race I had always wanted to win, from the time I did that first mini-marathon all those years back. It meant such a lot to me. It also gave me a lot of confidence – showed me that I could do it, that there was a future in the sport for me.

It was also a bit of a reality check. Stupidly, perhaps, I thought winning that marathon would change my life. I thought I had done it and I was now going to be a superstar. But it never happened. At first, I got phone calls saying I might get this sponsorship deal and that sponsorship deal. But after a month it all died down. There was no sponsorship deal. No Nike knocking on the door. People don't realise it. Even your family don't realise how it works. That it's just not like it is for the runners. Certainly not back then.

Jenny had been such a crucial figure in getting me to the top of the podium that day. Getting her back on board as coach had been a masterstroke. But it wasn't always plain sailing. When I went back to her, she was already working with another top British athlete called Tushar Patel. During those first few months I kept my head down. I didn't want to rock the boat. I just turned up, trained and went home. I did everything Jenny asked me to do in the sessions and having a quality training partner like Tush really gave the training a competitive edge which pushed us both on. Jenny never showed either of us preferential treatment. Everyone was the same.

Despite that there were obviously moments when the rivalry spilled over. In the build-up to the summer's World Championships in Lille she could obviously sense that something was wrong and that it was affecting our training. Jenny went absolutely mental at both of us, swearing loads: 'If you want to go to these Championships and represent your country then you better pull your finger out.'

I knew what she could be like when she got angry. She was used to working in a man's world so she had to be tough when needed. She did it to get in my mind. She was saying to me, do you really want this? I went home that night really scared – I didn't want to lose her as she had helped me so much over the years. I rang her up that night and said, 'Sorry, I really want your help.' She said, 'All right then, see you tomorrow.' That was the end of the matter. No recriminations or grudges. Done and dusted.

And so after that row they went their separate ways and I got one-on-ones with Jenny and got better and better.

Despite being so close to her and seeing her as another mother figure in my life I didn't tell Jenny about the recreational drugs for years. It wasn't until 2009 that I finally confessed all. I can remember exactly where we were, at the Robin Hood Gate in Richmond Park. I don't know why it came out then but it just did. I didn't know how she would react to it. But she was fantastic about it.

'What's done is done,' she said. 'You're not doing it now, are you?'

I told her no. 'Then you should move on. Are you glad you told me?'

By this point I was nearly in tears. I just felt so ashamed at what I had done. But it was a massive weight off my chest. It had been crushing me for so long and if I was really going to achieve everything I wanted then I had to be open and honest with her.

'As far as I am concerned it's over with. Yes, it was wrong, but these things happen.'

I just wished I had told her before. I know she would have reacted in the same way if I had done that right at the start. But it was all too raw then. It was too emotional for me.

As I headed to France for the World Championships I felt like my life was back on track. I had won the marathon and I felt in really good shape again.

I was just so proud to be back competing for my country – something I just hadn't believed was possible after all those dark years in the wilderness. It was hardly a glorious return, though. I wasn't selected for the 100m and finished just outside the medals in fourth place in the 200m and 400m. I felt so sure I was going to win a medal of some sort. When I failed to get anything I was so angry that I told the coach, Tanni's husband Ian Thompson, 'That's it. I am giving up sprinting.' I really lost it. I could have given up then. I thought, 'I am never going to medal, I am never going to get to Athens.' Some people might have been happy with fourth. But not me. I felt let down again.

———

One of the biggest fears any disabled person has is that their disability might affect their chances of having kids. Or – if they are lucky enough to be able to have children – that their disability will be passed onto them. I was no different. And until Kaylie got pregnant with Ronie in the early part of 2002, I was convinced I would never be a dad. I don't know why. The doctors had at no point in my life suggested that my condition might prevent me from having children. They kept telling me there was nothing in the family history to base my concerns on. I still had my doubts.

Kaylie and I hadn't been trying for Ronie. It was just one of those things that happened. I don't think Kaylie was too happy at first – she was only nineteen – but she obviously grew to love it. I was twenty-four and it felt like the right thing to be a dad.

Kaylie's pregnancy went pretty smoothly. There were no big scares. But her labour with Ronie was long. As any father knows, the wait is agonising. You feel so helpless. It was about twenty hours before my beautiful little girl emerged into the world, on 9 February 2003, at the same hospital where I had been born. The pride was overwhelming. I felt so honoured and relieved to be a dad. It also made me feel really grown up. Suddenly I was faced with a whole load of new responsibilities. We didn't know it was going to be a girl. We didn't find out because I didn't care; all I cared about was that the baby was healthy.

Throughout Kaylie's pregnancy with Ronie – and Emily's two with Mason and Tilly – I was always asking the midwife to do checks to see if the baby's spine was OK. It was always fine but with each of my children I have been worried sick that the doctors might have missed something. Until I can see with my own eyes that they are fine then I just don't believe it. I just didn't want any of my children to have anything wrong with them.

It was even worse with Mason. It's hard to explain but it is different with boys. Having a son is always special for the dad but I worried more that Mason might have problems. I just wanted him to be running around. Because I could always see that in my mum and dad's eyes. They probably wished I had been given that chance to run around – not just for them, but for me. Now when I see Mason running and jumping I can't contain my delight and relief. It's the same with all three of them. It just puts a smile on my face. Whenever Ronie and Mason come down to the track together and they start playing I just sit there and watch, trying to appreciate how lucky I am to have kids without any disabilities. As I watch Mason, my little boy, I imagine that's me, running around.

Of course that's not the end of the worries. If only. My fear now is, what if their kids are disabled? What if it skips a generation? If you look at me and Paul there has got to be something on my mum's side. You just don't know how the genes may be passed on down the generations. My case might have just been bad luck. I hope so because I would be devastated if it happened to my children as parents.

Coping with Ronie's arrival wasn't too bad. We both adjusted pretty well to being young parents. Like most people, we didn't have enough money and it was a bit of a struggle. But we made do and she certainly didn't go without.

Sometimes it was tough, especially in the first two months. All the screaming and sleepless nights. When you are not used to it and you have been doing double train-ing sessions it's really hard. But you just deal with it. And I never let it affect my training. After a while Ronie started to sleep through the night and things started to settle down. It was only a year to Athens and I had to get my qualifying times that summer.

After the World Championships in Lille, Jenny told me to keep training and working hard. So, having calmed down after the disappointment of coming fourth twice, that's exactly what I did. I changed a few things in the winter and I trained really hard. I had to accept that on this long road to the top I might have to get used to coming fourth and fifth before I could make the big breakthrough. That winter I worked tirelessly on my sprinting. I prioritised that over the London Marathon that year, which explains why I wasn't able to defend my title. But it paid dividends when the track season came around. I got my qualifying standards for Athens in the summer of 2003. Getting to Athens was the only thing I was focused on. I kept the painful experience of watching Sydney on the TV as my main motivation, the driving force behind my dreams.

As the Games got closer and closer I remember all the media focus was on the Greeks' preparations. Would they be ready in time? Was it going to be a shambles? But I didn't care about all that. I just wanted to get there and race – whatever state Athens was in. The call eventually came in July from Ian Thompson, head of the British athletics team. He told me I had been selected because of my form and performances over the last two years. This was an incredible moment for me. Ever since I had turned my back on the sport, deep down I had doubted whether I would get another chance to go to a Paralympic Games. It's one of the great contradictions of elite sportsmen and women. Confidence is such a big part of success and when I am out on the track I am totally in control, completely sure of myself. But away from the heat of battle it's a never-ending struggle against my own mind. My fears and doubts. They are always there and, having gone through the worst few years of my young life, I wasn't sure I would get my second chance.

Before the Games started the British team flew off to Cyprus for a training camp. We had about three weeks left to fine-tune our preparations, to fix any last-minute problems and to acclimatise to the heat of the late Greek summer. In keeping with the shoddy image of the Athens Games, the track we were supposed to use in Nicosia wasn't ready – I don't know why, but it was a real shame. So we ended up using this rubbish track in Paphos. It was way too soft and I had to change all my training plans by switching to the road instead, something I really didn't want to do just before my first Paralympics for eight years.

Fortunately, I was flying in training. Jenny had been timing me in the sessions. She refused to tell me how fast I was going – she didn't want me to get complacent. While it tears me apart inside, she knows a few self-doubts are good for me in the long run. They make me work even harder. But I just had this feeling I was going well, that I was ready.

Watching the Olympics earlier in the summer had given me a taste of what to expect when we arrived in the Greek capital. By this time the bigger worries about the venues and the transport had gone away. OK, so it was a bit rough and ready around the edges but the history of the place more than made up for that. Everywhere you looked there was some ancient ruin or other and it was a genuine privilege to be competing in a Games where the Olympic ideal had been born. I thought the place was very special.

In the village there was a great atmosphere, such a contrast to my first experience in Atlanta. The Greeks treated us really well. It was a bit of a journey from the village to the stadium but as long as you planned it well, it wasn't too much of a problem. The food was great compared to Atlanta and for me that made a massive difference. The track in the village was first class and there was a 50-metre pool to play in. They did a decent job. The rooms were pretty good and I was sharing with Lloyd Upsdell, a cerebral palsy athlete who'd won two golds in Sydney four years earlier. He was from Essex, so, as you might imagine, there was a fair bit of banter. We had a laugh and looked after each other. He was a good teammate and I missed him when he retired from the sport.

The only disappointment was the size of the crowds. Again, as with Atlanta, the IPC and the organisers had not promoted the Paralympics properly. It was obvious the Greeks just weren't into it in the same way as the Australian public had been in Sydney in 2000. But the IPC didn't help themselves by scheduling big races – like the blue riband event, the 1,500m – at nine in the morning. How do they expect people to come out and support Paralympic sport, especially in a country known to be lukewarm to anything other than football and basketball? You don't do that. You put it at prime time in the evening. I will never understand how the IPC comes to make these decisions. They don't talk to athletes. But this time I wasn't going to let it ruin my experience. I had grown up a lot over the last eight years and with London's bid for the 2012 Games already under way, I was confident future Paralympics could and would be different.

On the start line of the qualifying heat for the 200m my heart was racing so fast that when the announcer called out my name my GB vest was throbbing.

I ignored the rows of empty seats. 'Who cares?' I thought. 'This is my moment and I am going to make the most of it.'

Afterwards, when I looked at the time, it was the second fastest in qualifying. Suddenly a medal was realistic. This was a game changer.

In the final I was nervous – really nervous. Eight years ago I had tasted what it was like to be in a Paralympic final and I had been happy not to come last. Now, suddenly, I was in with a chance of getting on the podium, of winning my first medal. Realistically, I knew I would struggle to win gold, but if I could just stay in contention with the big guns I might be in the mix.

When the starter went off, everything went perfectly. As I expected, Leo-Pekka Tähti was too fast and won in world-record time. Kenny van Weeghel of Holland came second, but I managed to hold on for bronze. That was all I wanted. My first real taste of success. That night, I was so excited I couldn't sleep. I just kept looking at the medal, reliving the race and the moment on the podium.

After I got back to the village I was on the phone for hours talking to my family. No mobiles in those days: I had to buy a phone card and go and use the public phone.

The problem was that next morning I had my heats for the 400m. I didn't even qualify. I was just so tired and exhausted. But I was so happy. Ever since I went off the rails I had imagined how it would feel to hold a Paralympic medal in my hands. Now, to have that sense of achievement was better than taking any recreational drug. All the goings-on over the previous few years just vanished. But, like any drug, success leaves you wanting more.

My experience in the 400m had been a blow but at least I had another chance to make amends in the 100m. Jenny told me to forget about what had happened; she said I had simply got overexcited. I hadn't expected to get a medal so it was totally understandable. She is so good like that, putting everything into perspective, especially when you are worried you might have let yourself down. Then she told me the truth about how fast I had been going in training. I thought the 100m was my weakest event. But she was the one with the stopwatch and she saw a very different athlete to the one I had in my head. It was a great tactic, to wait until the last couple of days before the heats and then give me that lift by telling me how fast I had been going over the distance in training.

Normally, once you are in a big competition like a Paralympics you don't tend to lift heavy weights. But I just wanted to do a little session before the 100m. Just like for the able-bodied sprinters, psychology over the short, explosive sprint races is massively important. If you look ripped and your arm muscles are bulging on the start line then it can help put a doubt in your opponents' minds. Jenny was a bit unsure. She was worried I might do myself some harm. So I was restricted to just twenty minutes in the gym. But it gave me such a boost. It was a little thing but it made such a big difference to my confidence.

When it came to the night of the heats I was watching the early rounds from the tunnel in the stadium. Each race was over in fourteen seconds but it felt like a lifetime. As each heat passed so a new Paralympic record was being set. Everyone was flying. I was thinking, 'Oh my God, what have I got to do to even get to the second round?'

When I crossed the line in my heat I couldn't believe it. I smashed the Paralympic record. I was the fastest out of everyone.

'Oh my God, what have I just done?'

What an achievement – my first major record. 14.16 seconds. Now I was really pumped. I came through the semi-final and booked my place in the final alongside the best sprinters in the world. I was in lane four, next to my old roommate from Atlanta, Dave Holding. He was thirty-five now and in his last Games. But even his presence didn't calm my nerves. I was absolutely terrified. Two false starts helped. Most sprinters don't like them as it puts them on edge, slows them down. But I like them. I am not the best starter in the world so anything which keeps me in contention in the early stages of the race gives me a chance when my power and top-end speed come into play towards the finish line. I rolled back slowly. I remember thinking, 'Don't go off too fast.' The gun went and I absolutely nailed it. I crossed the line in second place, winning my first silver medal. To be just one away from gold – it was such an honour for me. Athens will always have a special place in my heart because it was all so new, so unexpected. I am not normally one for keeping memorabilia or collecting stuff but I have kept a lot of things from 2004.

I was so grateful to Jenny. It was a massive achievement and she had done so much to help me turn things around. I had gone to Athens just to be part of the British set-up once more, to repay people I had let down back in 1998 when I didn't show up for the World Championships. To come out of those dark days and be there, I felt like I had done myself justice. I felt very lucky and felt as if I had angels around me looking after me. When I was on the podium getting those two medals I just kept thanking everyone in my mind – my parents, Jenny, my brothers and now my little girl, Ronie. My mum and dad were obviously bursting with pride. My mates arranged a huge party when I returned, at the Windmill, the local pub on Roundshaw. It was such a shock to me, I didn't expect it at all. But to share my success with all the people I had grown up with, and on the estate, who had always supported me was really special. Now it is my regular celebration venue whenever the all-conquering hero returns from the Games.

Athens had not reaffirmed my faith in the Paralympics, but it had shown me what I could achieve if I put my mind to it. I had come close to squandering my talent. I could have thrown it all away for a life drifting around and being angry at my fate. Instead, I felt like I was the lucky one. The one with the gift. The Games convinced me I had been right to go back to racing and to get myself straight. But very soon after I returned, my mind was already turning to the next goal and the next four years. Even though sprinting had brought me my first real taste of success I didn't want to carry on over those distances. I wanted a bigger challenge, I wanted to really push myself. And now I wanted to taste what it was like to win gold.

CHAPTER 6

BREAKING BOUNDARIES

Any athlete, able bodied or disabled, will tell you that medals are all that matter. That winning is what really counts. But breaking world records? Well, that's a totally different buzz. Addictive. Infectious. Until you've done it, it's hard to explain. But once you've got one world record under your belt, you want to keep breaking them, pushing the boundaries and setting new standards.

This was the phase my career was now entering as I emerged from Athens a more rounded and confident athlete. I felt I had put my past firmly behind me. I had done my growing up. Now I was ready to really take on the world, to push on and see how far – and how fast – I could go.

I also had the ultimate incentive. On 6 July 2005 Jacques Rogge, the president of the International Olympic Committee (IOC), uttered the words that would change my life forever.

'And the Games of the 30th Olympiad in 2012 are awarded to the city of … London.'

A home Games: the ultimate incentive. After a two-year campaign which culminated in a meeting of the IOC in Singapore, London had won. We had seen off favourites Paris and serious contenders Madrid. What had seemed like a long shot had suddenly become very real. The Paralympics would be happening in my home town.

Most people were crowded around TVs and radios waiting for the announcement, but not me. I had been competing in Switzerland and was waiting for a flight back to London when the news was relayed over the airport Tannoy system. It felt strange being away at such a big moment for the country – it just made me want to get home even faster. When I eventually did see a TV report I remember seeing Danny Crates, my Paralympic teammate, going nuts at a big event in Trafalgar Square after the decision. They kept playing it back again and again. It was hilarious. Then there were the great scenes from Singapore – Seb Coe and Ken Livingstone looking slightly stunned, Tanni Grey-Thompson being hugged by Sir Keith Mills, and Becks just beaming. At that moment my training went up a gear. I had the biggest incentive to do well and I knew that if I got my training right and worked hard I would be coming into my peak.

I am such a proud Brit – I guess it comes from my dad's army days when he served in the Irish Guards – so to host the Olympics and Paralympics meant the world to me. We had to get it right. We couldn't screw it up.

With London 2012 acting as a new motivational force,

the next two years saw a transformation in my racing career. I set new world records in the 800m, 5,000m and – most precious of all – the 1,500m, the blue riband of wheelchair racing. It was an incredible time, a period of my career I thought I would never better.

After winning my first Paralympic medals in Athens I was the man to watch on the circuit. I now had two years to get ready for the 2006 World Championships in the Dutch town of Assen. The year after Athens was pretty laid-back. I had worked so hard to get to the Games that I figured I could take my foot off the pedal for a year. But come the winter I was ready to get back into my training. I was desperate to move on from the sprint events and into the tougher, more tactical territory of middle-distance racing.

For the one and only time in my career, the set-up at UK Athletics (UKA), the sport's governing body, worked for me rather than against me. The Australian Kathryn Periac had become the performance manager for wheelchair athletes at UKA, a move I was really pleased with. She was a former athlete herself and knew I had been through a lot of problems in the past with UKA. They didn't believe in me and hadn't helped me and Jenny. In our first meeting I told her everything and explained how I wanted to move up to the middle distances. She said, 'OK, I will fund you,' but asked that I leave the door open for some of the sprinting events. I agreed. It was such a breath of fresh air and the start of the best period I enjoyed with UKA. Overseeing it all was Tim Jones, who was an amazing manager, and working with Kathryn was Pete Wyman, brought in as the head coach for wheelchair athletes. He was a former runner and understood the sport inside out. He got round all the top athletes, asking how he and UKA could help. But he never interfered with Jenny and the way we worked together. He let Jenny get on with it. It was exactly the set-up I needed. But trying to deliver on that commitment to carry on in the sprints and move on to the middle distances I wanted to compete in was not going to be easy. Fortunately, I was in the form of my life.

2006 was my invincible year. I was simply unbeatable. And in that sort of shape, world records were going to fall.

The first two of my career came in one very special night, in Ibach in Switzerland. It was high up in the mountains and I remember it was absolutely perfect conditions: really high, thin clouds and no wind or rain. I was going for the 400m and the 200m and my training had been going really well but in the longer distance I knew I always died in the last few metres. Jenny and I had worked really hard on getting it right. So when the race started I knew I was going to break the world record. Just looking at the speedometer on my chair I knew I was flying – I was doing 21mph on the straights.

As I crossed the line I looked over at the clock: 46.89 seconds – my first world record. I remember Tanni was there and she was so made up. You could see in her eyes how excited she was. I didn't have a phone and I wanted to call Jenny so Tanni lent me hers so I could break the news to her. She was obviously delighted but it was a brief call as I had to go and get ready for the 200m.

And an hour or so later I smashed the 200m world record as well. I have never been near those times since. It was just a perfect day. No one had been under 25 seconds in the 200m for six years. It was unreal. I just couldn't believe it was happening to me. The fastest man in the world? I saw the change among my rivals: instant respect. What made it even more satisfying was that I didn't even want the 200m. I didn't think it was a good event for me.

The 1,500m was the one I really wanted. That summer I started racing over the distance and I was rewriting the rulebook. The races always used to start and build up slowly. But I went from the off. And all the regulars over the distance weren't used to that. Soon I was going under three minutes and I knew that when that happened it was only a matter of time until that world record was mine. I was getting stronger and stronger. The other guys could see how much I was improving. They knew it wasn't a fluke. Stepping up the distances suited me.

But for all my record-breaking exploits, hardly anyone was paying attention. No wheelchair racer expects to get the same attention as when Seb Coe broke his three world records inside forty-one days back in 1979, but you would think it might get a mention in one of the papers. My friends and family obviously knew and were made up, but the public had no idea. It was a bit frustrating. I was really making a name for myself and yet I didn't have any big sponsors and I was on B funding – the lower level of National Lottery support – because I still hadn't won a gold medal.

When I broke the 200m and 400m world records in Switzerland that day, you know what I won? A Swiss army knife. No prize money, no appearance money. Nothing. Now, I accept that as a Paralympian you aren't going to get the same sort of cash as the able-bodied athletes and over-all I try not to let these things bother me too much. But I do think meeting promoters should find a way of incentivising athletes like me to break world records.

With things going so well, I approached that year's World Championships with real anticipation. But I also had a big dilemma. UKA had agreed to let me explore the longer distances on the condition I didn't turn my back on sprinting. Faced with such a punishing schedule in Assen, I knew something had to give. I couldn't do six events and realistically stand a chance of winning. At one stage I was contemplating doing the 100m, 200m, 400m, 800m, 1,500m and 5,000m.

Maybe I should explain here why wheelchair athletes like me are even able to consider racing over such a wide range of distances. Unlike able-bodied runners, who can run faster over shorter distances, wheelchair racers build more slowly towards their top speeds and can then maintain a decent pace for much longer distances. It's still a question of stamina, but providing you have a good technique and conserve energy for the sprint finishes at the end it's a bit like being the Duracell bunny. We just go on and on. It's one of the strange quirks of wheelchair athletics that the average speed in a marathon – a race of 26.2 miles – is higher than in a long-distance track race. That's mainly because on the track you have to negotiate bends and all the bunching that goes with racing on a tight circuit. But in a road race like a marathon you don't have tight turns and you have the luxury of much more space.

But even allowing for all that, contemplating all these events was stupid – the timetable of heats and finals would have been impossible to manage. In the end, I dropped the 5,000m – I wasn't ready.

However, while it might have been too soon to move on to the longest track distance, I also had good reason not to turn my back on the shortest: revenge.

It was May 2006 and I was in Switzerland for a 100m race. It was a good field, which summed up what a strong period this was for wheelchair sprinting. There was Kenny van Weeghel, the Flying Dutchman, who won gold over 200m in the World Championships in 2003 and then gold in the 400m in Athens in 2004. The Finn Leo-Pekka Tähti was also in the line-up. Leo is really quiet off the track but on it he's a monster. He was undoubtedly the man to beat, having won gold in the 100m and 200m at the Athens Paralympics. Wheelchair racing needed big names and big characters, and these were two of the biggest names around – I was honoured to be competing with guys like this.

But just because I respected them, that didn't mean that

I had to turn a blind eye if I felt they were doing something wrong. As we all waited for the gun to go in that 100m that night, Kenny got off to an absolute flyer. He roared away to win the race and smash Leo's world record. Afterwards I was so angry. I was absolutely convinced Kenny had jumped the gun. And that gave Kenny an unfair advantage. So I asked the officials, 'How on earth can you let that stand?'

Kenny tried to tough it out. 'Look, whatever happened has now happened. What can I do about it?'

But I didn't let it go. And after the officials looked again at the replay of the race they saw he had false-started and disqualified him. Leo's record stood and justice had been done. But I was still angry about the way Kenny had reacted. If he had put his hands up then that might have been different. He is normally a nice bloke but that went against the spirit of the sport. I told Jenny afterwards that I would do the 100m at the World Championships one last time. I wanted to win gold and deny Kenny in his home country.

Fast-forward a few months to Kenny's backyard, the De Smelt Arena, and the World Championships 100m final. I hadn't forgotten about what had happened a few months earlier in Switzerland, and I was determined to get my own back. In the end it was a tight race but I did it, beating him by a couple of hundredths of a second. It was a fantastic feeling – not only to be world champion but to beat Kenny. To me, he hadn't held up his hands. If you lose you lose.

Take it on the chin and work harder and make sure you don't get beaten again.

I have a reputation on the circuit for being a bit ruthless and I know people are scared of me. They know I won't take any nonsense on the track. If I make a mistake or knock people then I will hold my hands up and apologise, but others try and put you off deliberately. The most common bit of gamesmanship in wheelchair athletics is to try and knock your opponents' hands. It's a bit like when runners catch the back of their rivals' heels. Wheelchair racing is all about maintaining a steady rhythm. You need to keep pumping your arms up and down, pushing down on the rims which drive your two back wheels. If someone knocks your hand it can disturb that rhythm and give them an advantage.

Racing chairs have come a long way in the last twenty years but they are still extremely difficult to steer around a track. Each one has its own steering lever above the main frame which runs down to the front wheel. But because you want to maintain your speed and momentum you don't want to cruise around the bend holding the lever and not pushing your back wheels. So you can set your chair to two different modes – the straight and the bend. The wheels then lock to the right angle for both sections of the track and all you have to do is to hit the compensator, another lever which sits under the frame, to flick between the two.

This means that going into and out of the bends we are

all leaning forward to whack our compensators and at that point you can – accidentally or otherwise – knock your opponents' hands as they are trying to push. Of course, whenever you confront someone about it they will tell you it's not deliberate. But I am not so sure. If someone knocks my gloves when my arms are in full flow, I simply give them a look. They know not to do it again.

What I do know is that I don't do it deliberately to other people. I have never had anyone say I race unfairly. I have never seen any remarks from anyone saying I was dirty. All right, I might be aggressive: you have to be to win. I don't take any nonsense from anyone. I am there to race. There are no rules and regulations about racing aggressively. If you can't take it then don't do it. If someone wants to sit behind you for the whole race then deal with it. It's just racing, isn't it? There's nothing in the rulebook that says you have to take the front. That's why I always try and keep out of trouble. What I do is keep my front wheel on the outside of my fiercest rival's back wheels otherwise I could get stuck. For years and years Jenny has taught me that technique. Then, if you need to get out, you can. You want to avoid getting boxed in at all costs.

People might be surprised to learn that wheelchair athletes are as competitive and ruthless as we are. But this is world-class elite sport. It's just like running, but with chairs instead. I never back down. Someone will have to. But it's not going to be me.

Of course, all this can lead to some pretty nasty crashes.

Perhaps the most infamous came in the women's 5,000m in my classification – the T54 – during the Beijing 2008 Games. You can see the video on YouTube. It was really messy. With two laps to go everyone was really tightly bunched when, all of a sudden, the two Swiss athletes leading the pack clashed wheels. They hit the deck, causing nearly everyone just behind them to crash too. It was almost a total wipe-out. Officials then ran onto the track, impeding those athletes who did manage to avoid the crash. One of the athletes broke her collarbone and, although they awarded the medals, the race had to be rerun following an appeal.

It just shows how wheelchair racing is not for the faint-hearted. But I am not frightened of the dangers and what might happen on the track. I don't even think about it. It's all part of the sport.

After winning the 100m I went from strength to strength. The only event I didn't win was the 200m, where I got a silver. I left Assen that September with four gold medals and that one silver. It was my big breakthrough. That season I was unbeatable.

———

Looking back on that period of my career, I find it quite difficult to believe what I achieved. Because, away from the track, my life was a mess. I have no idea how I broke those records and won those gold medals. Mentally, I just wasn't there. I couldn't even train properly. Sometimes I would spend the first hour in Richmond Park just crying.

By the early part of 2006 my relationship with Kaylie had broken down. It had become impossible for us to live with each other. Maybe it was because her nan died around that time. Or maybe it was because we got together when she was too young. But whatever the reason, it became a living hell for me.

I was always grateful for what she had done for me seven years before. Without her I might not even be here to write this story. But we changed so much that there was no option but to end it and to go our separate ways.

I had experienced failing relationships in the past and I knew how painful they could be. But this was different. This time there was a child caught up in it all. For Ronie, who was almost three when it all came to a head, it was a terrible time. Kaylie and I were rowing all the time and I felt she was going out too much. I never knew where she was. That year I was on the road more than ever before. I was racing as much as I could and would spend long periods away. I was trying to succeed in the career she had encouraged me to go into and to make some money for the family. I just thought if I could break through and do well in the future maybe I would be able to look after everyone. And yet every time I left the country I was worrying about what might be going on back home.

Perhaps she felt she needed to get something out of her system. Maybe she got tied down with me too young and wasn't really ready to handle all my problems. All I do know is that that year was such a struggle for me at home. I just didn't trust her.

At the time I was devastated. I felt it was me. I felt because I was devoting so much time to my career, it must be my fault. I was insecure because I was in a wheelchair. But in fairness to Kaylie my disability had never been an issue. She said it just didn't bother her that I was in a wheelchair. It's been like that with a lot of the girls I have had relationships with over the years. They just don't see me in that way. They look past the chair. It never created any tension that we couldn't always do the same things as other couples. There was never any sense of resentment. I think we just fell in love too young and that she wanted a different life. I remember ringing her all the time when I was in Holland for the World Championships and most of the time she wasn't even in. That just drove me mad. It felt like my life was just falling apart.

I felt very alone. I couldn't rely on my friends as they didn't warm to Kaylie. And so it was Jenny I turned to. She was the only person I could really talk to about it. She told me her door was always open. She even offered to take care of Ronie if I needed her to.

In the back of my mind I kept thinking about those dark days. I didn't want to go back there. I knew I was stronger now. I was enjoying the success of racing and I didn't want to do anything to jeopardise that ever again – even if it did mean breaking up with Kaylie. So I threw myself into my sport, training harder and harder. Sometimes I would be up all night but I would go and train the next day as hard as I could. At first the breakdown had upset my training. But I had done my crying.

As for women, well, I didn't like them much after that. I lost total respect for them. Not my mum or Jenny – they were strong women and I had been surrounded by strong women my whole life. But this really shook my confidence.

The end came shortly after I returned from Holland. Jenny gave me ten days off, so I was at home a lot. For the first time I could see with my own eyes what had really been happening. One night Kaylie told me she was going out to some bar or club. She told me not to expect her to be back until the small hours. When she eventually came back in the middle of the night, we had a massive argument. Ronie was crying her heart out. Kaylie just got up and left.

Unable to call my mum, the first person I rang was my dad. He was in Ireland so wasn't really in a position to do much about it. But I just needed to talk to someone. I was so low. My dad told me the first thing I should do was to get my mum round and talk to her. So I lay in bed for a few hours before I plucked up the courage to ring her. It was the first time we had spoken in months and that was a very long time for us as we had always been so close.

I could accept that Kaylie might not want to be with me. But the thing that really killed me was the thought of someone else bringing up Ronie. Another man playing her dad. So I tried to make it work, tried to argue that we should stay together. I wanted to protect Ronie. She was so little, way too young to understand what was happening to her mum and dad.

But Kaylie wanted to move on. So, in the autumn of 2006, we split for good.

The first four or five months were really tough. Kaylie stayed at our place and I went back to my mum's with Alfie, my Staffordshire bull terrier. I have always been a dog lover and have three of them now. Alfie had to come with me, though my mum needed some convincing, not about me but about Alfie. Ironically, when things settled down and I moved out again, Alfie stayed with her.

At the time it was nice to move back; I couldn't stay in our house. Even when Kaylie moved back to her mum's house, I couldn't go back there for months. It just had so many bad memories. I only moved back after my mate Leon said he would come and stay with me for two or three nights a week, to make sure I was OK. I needed some-one with me all the time at that stage because that house felt quite lonely. Even Alfie wouldn't come back with me. Even now I can still feel the bad times in that place. It's especially bad for Emily, who has to share a house with my past. We are desperate to move on and find a place we can really call our own. A place not haunted by that fractured relationship.

As I threw myself into my racing and training, my friends tried to tell me not to worry: 'You'll get over it,' they kept saying.

I didn't believe them. And then one day, around Christmas time, it just happened. Someone mentioned her name and it suddenly didn't bother me. That's when I knew I had moved on. It made me smile inside. In the past I would have been upset about it and cut up. It was quicker than I expected but I was ready to start again.

Even now, Kaylie and I still do not have a good relationship. For Ronie I think the whole set-up, with me in one place with another partner and her mum in another place living with someone else, has robbed her of a big part of her childhood. I see Ronie two or three times a week and she comes and stays with me, mostly during the week.

The whole situation with Kaylie hadn't been made any easier by the fact that my parents also broke up that year. It was very sad but it didn't have too much of an impact on me. Maybe I was too preoccupied with my own break-up. Maybe I was too old to be affected by it. By this stage I was big enough and ugly enough to know that if my mum and dad weren't getting on then they should move on. They were still friends but they had just grown apart. They wanted to have different lives.

My dad went back to Northern Ireland but there were no arguments and it wasn't a horrible environment. It was peaceful. My brothers were a bit gutted as he had brought them up as if they were his own sons. He had also been my mum's rock. They tried to tell her not to let him go. But no one could make them stay together. We were all old enough to deal with it, all over twenty. It was such a shame, though. They had been together for over thirty years.

At that stage my dad wasn't really part of my racing career. Out of habit he would always ring to check up on me and ask if I had been training. It was a habit.

'Yes, Dad, I am training,' I would tell him. It was as if I was still ten years old. But I love him for that.

———

As 2007 dawned I was ready to make a fresh start. Just after the New Year I headed to Australia for some warm-weather training. I had a phone but I didn't use it. I wanted to just concentrate on my training and getting fit for the new season. It was going to be a big year. The 2008 Beijing Games were just around the corner and I knew I had to be on top of my game one year out to ensure I got all the qualifying times under my belt.

I also had an appointment with a certain world record. Having set the new standard in the 200m and 400m the previous year, I now wanted that 1,500m mark. That was the one I really wanted. Even though I had trained for it from the start of the year, all through the winter months and into the spring, I always thought it was an impossible target. It had been broken at a Diamond League meeting in Zurich in early 2000. A kilo of gold was up for grabs then, so some of the top guys got together to break the record and then split the money. That would have been a decent purse for Paralympic athletes so it was a big incentive.

When my chance came to break it there was no purse of gold involved, or field of big guns with a pacemaker, all put together to beat the clock. And of all the places to break this treasured record it turned out to be in Atlanta, the city which had left me feeling so disenchanted with the sport all those years ago. I had already raced in one meeting up on the east coast of the States, in Long Island. Then I headed south for my date with destiny. It was late June and when I got off the plane in Atlanta it was absolutely red-hot. It was a tiny little venue – it's not even there now – and it was a world away from the Olympic Stadium used for the 1996 Games. But it had a very fast track.

Because of the heat we had to wait until late in the evening to race. About ten minutes before the start, I could sense the conditions would be perfect. No wind, a bit of light rain, but really steamy and warm. Everything felt just right. So I decided there and then: I was going to go for the world record.

I told Josh George, an American athlete, to stay behind me because I was going for a good time. I went from the gun and I did lap after lap from the front of the field. In the middle stage I slowed up a bit. I started to panic. I thought I had blown my chance. So, on the final lap I really went for it. As I crossed the line I could hear the American commentator going absolutely crazy. It was a total blur but when I looked at the clock I realised what I had done.

2 minutes 55.25 seconds – a new world record.

I was so thrilled at what I had done. It was the record I had always wanted. And I had done it without it all being set up for me. That was important to me. I wanted to prove you could break records on your own. It was probably one of my best-ever races – if not *the* best. To do that on your own and drive your way through and set a world record – it was an unbelievable feeling.

There was no crowd there really. It was a small meeting for disabled athletes and part of the wheelchair racing world series. I used to travel the world to get points and for the winner at the end of the season there was a bit of prize money. But it was only about $3,000 – hardly life changing. By the time you had bought flights to get to all these meetings and paid for your hotels and food you were well out of pocket. But I didn't worry about that then. I was just so into my racing. It was great to race around the world, and to break that record made me so proud. I couldn't wait to tell people.

But I wasn't finished yet. Later that night I had to go again, this time in the 5,000m. There were quite a few big racers in the field so, with qualifying times for Beijing on our minds, we agreed to get together and help each other. I was sharing the workload with my Australian rival Kurt Fearnley, taking it in turns to push on the pace. But the track in Atlanta, while fast, was also very tight and I was wheel-spinning a lot. As the race wore on I dropped back to fifth place. At that stage Kurt was way out in front and

I only had 300 metres to go. I had to go right out to lane four, halfway across this track, just to get through all the traffic. I thought I had left it too late but I was in such good shape, moving so fast. As I came off the final bend I was just gaining and gaining on him and when I crossed the line I thought, 'I've got this.'

It was so tight the officials had to call for a photo finish. But deep down I knew I had got the win – and another world record.

9 minutes 53.15 seconds. I was the first man to go under ten minutes.

The record had stood for about a decade – back to the time when the great Mexican Saúl Mendoza was on top of his game. I had broken two world records in one night. And I hadn't even been racing in the 5,000m for very long. That was what made me realise that I had to move up to the longer distances and leave sprinting behind. Beijing was now just a year away and, for all the problems I had experienced with Kaylie, my racing had never been better – I was the best in the world, unbeatable. For the first time in my life I felt like things were really starting to go my way.

CHAPTER 7

THE BATTLE OF BEIJING

I was always scared of going to China. I had heard all the stories. The way the Chinese treated people in wheelchairs. How some disabled people ended up as slaves. How they lived and died in terrible poverty, ignored by the rest of society. Could China really host a Paralympic Games? A celebration of the kind of people the country seemed to want to hide from public view?

My first visit there in May, just four months before the Games, confirmed my fears. It was a Paralympic test event, a warm-up for the real act to come later in the year. But for me it wasn't just about getting a sneak preview of the Bird's Nest (the Beijing National Stadium), the track or the Olympic Park. I wanted to get a feel for what China and Beijing were all about.

As I travelled around that week, I kept an eye out for other disabled people. You did see older people in wheelchairs but apart from that I didn't see a single disabled person. People looked at you as if you were something from another planet. It was actually quite frightening.

Then there was the pollution. A thick smog hung over Beijing and I was getting nosebleeds. I had travelled over to China with Kathryn Periac. Once I told her about the nosebleeds she told me not to worry about training or the race. Just see it as a fact-finding mission. The day after I won my test event race in the magnificent Bird's Nest I went back on day two to watch some of the athletics and I saw what looked like a trail of little footprints on the track. But it was nowhere near the sand pits for the jumps. Where was it coming from? Then I realised. It was the smog lying on the track.

'Oh my God,' I thought. 'I am killing myself being here.'

Once you got out of the city it was a different story. One morning we drove out to see the Great Wall of China. I knew once the Games were on in September I wouldn't get a chance. I wouldn't want the distraction. So I took my opportunity to see the sights then – the Wall, the Forbidden City, Tiananmen Square. As we drove up towards the section of the Great Wall we had chosen, the thick fog lifted, the sky turned blue and I could breathe clean, fresh air. Some other things didn't change so quickly, though. Once there, it was almost impossible to get up onto the Wall in a wheelchair. We had to go up on these little cable cars which didn't look like the safest thing in the world. And of course I didn't see another soul in a wheelchair.

That experience definitely opened my mind to China a

bit more, gave me a much better understanding. But I still found it an intimidating place.

'When the Paralympics starts,' I thought to myself, 'there will be almost 4,000 disabled athletes here, people with limbs missing, people who can't talk properly, athletes on blades. What are they going to be like? How will the Chinese public react?'

I spoke to other Paralympians, who shared my concerns. They were a bit frightened by the smog and worried about the attitudes they might encounter. We just didn't know what to expect. It might have been the language barrier or the lack of openness, but China never really communicated to us what it was going to be like. From the moment I left Athens I had been wondering, 'Would the crowds turn up? Would it be well organised? Would they really care about the Paralympics?'

Everything else was amazing: on first inspection the stadiums and facilities were perfect, the best I had ever seen. And their Paralympic team was obviously full of fantastic athletes. Well, with a population of more than eighty million disabled people you would expect a bit of strength on their side. But would any of that make a difference?

———

Throughout 2006 and the early part of 2007 the road to Beijing had been extremely smooth. In fact, it had been the best period of my career. I had smashed two world records in Atlanta and I was looking forward to competing in the World Athletics Championships in the Japanese port city of Osaka in August 2007.

But then everything had gone wrong. After I had come back from the States, I felt very light-headed. Really funny and weird. It just wasn't right. I told Jenny and she gave me a week off. After eight days I still felt jet-lagged. That doesn't normally happen.

So I did a couple of training sessions and I said to Jen, 'I feel absolutely shattered.' I was sweating a lot and I couldn't get up to speed. She told me to go to my local GP and have a blood test. About a week later the results came back and they seemed OK. But I wasn't convinced. One of my glands was up, and I wondered if I just had a bad cold.

I went to see the Team GB doctors at St Mary's. I explained how I felt – tired, lethargic all the time. They did another blood test. The next day they came back and told me I had glandular fever. I panicked.

'Is there a pill to fix it?' I asked them.

'Afraid not, Dave,' they told me. 'There's no cure. All you can do is rest and after a few months you will feel better, although it can stay in your system for three years.'

'Three years?' I said. 'Are you serious? I've got Beijing next year. What am I going to do?' At that point I thought my chances of winning gold in Beijing had gone.

A week after that diagnosis I was supposed to be racing at Crystal Palace in the annual Diamond League meeting. It's always a big event for me. It's my local track and the fans know I come from round the corner. Now I had a big decision to make. I told Jenny I was going to race.

'Please let me race at Palace,' I said to Jenny. 'For my own peace of mind, let me do it.'

I raced there and I won. So I started to wonder whether I could go to Osaka after all. Maybe it wasn't that serious. That was when Jenny put her foot down. 'You can't go to Japan,' she said. 'You are going to seriously hurt yourself. You have got Beijing next year and just think about what you have got to do. What's the priority? Beijing could be a big year for you.'

That upset me. And then it just got worse. All I could do was take loads of vitamins and iron as there were no medicines or pills I could take to make it better. The doctors said it could have been caused by the stress I had been through the year before – all the ups and downs with Kaylie and the break-up. I then realised how badly I had been treating my body – not eating properly, all that travelling around the world chasing qualifying times and world records, all those stressful, scary flights. I was an emotional wreck. My body just blew up. It couldn't do it any more.

At the time I thought I was doing all the right things. I was so focused on doing well. I went out to the pub with my mates but I didn't drink alcohol. I would just go out to socialise and wouldn't stay out late – I would be home by 11 p.m. because I knew I had to get up for training. But during the split with Kaylie I couldn't just sit indoors on my own. It was too hard. I hadn't done that for years.

Now, though, my body was telling me another story. Some days I went to bed early and would sleep all the way through but when I woke up it felt like I hadn't slept a wink. I tried to train but in the end I had to pack it in. Through the crucial winter months of 2007–8 I didn't train at all.

UKA were very worried. Kathryn Periac, Tim Jones and the doctors were all monitoring me. They were doing lots of tests on me, blood and urine, and keeping all sorts of charts and records, trying to assess where my fitness was heading. They just told me rest was the best thing, to see if I could get it out of my system. My first target in 2008 was the London Marathon. Incredibly, despite the illness, I won. But it took a lot out of me and I was really ill afterwards. Whenever I peaked I really paid a heavy price. I would be wiped out for weeks. Add to that the fact that I couldn't eat properly: I would miss meals, get up and train. Just have a Red Bull and then go.

Diet is such an important part of being an elite athlete. But you can't eat properly all the time. It drives you mad. It's expensive too. Fresh fruit costs you a fortune, supplements are dear. When you aren't making that much money you cut corners on the things that can make such an enormous difference to your performance.

The one blessing from putting myself and my body under such strain in 2007 was that I had already got the qualifying times for all the distances I was considering going for in Beijing – the 100m, 200m, 400m, 800m, 1,500m, 5,000m and marathon! Having that range made me feel a bit better, because I could choose shorter distances if I wasn't feeling great.

After a short break in Ireland with my dad when I took Ronie over to meet my nan, her great-grandmother, for the first time, I worked out a training schedule which allowed for my glandular fever. I wasn't about to give up on Beijing, having spent the last two and a half years on top of the world. I knew this was the peak of my career, the time when I should have been at my strongest, and I couldn't guarantee that four years on in London I could still compete with the best.

I worked out I had about ten weeks when I could push it. I locked down the distances I was going to compete in, five events: the 400m, 800m, 1,500m, 5,000m and the marathon. It was a mad challenge at the best of times ... but when you are ill? Completely insane. But that was me. I had to do it. Of course, I didn't think I was going to win five gold medals. My theory was that if it went wrong in one I had got another opportunity. It was an insurance policy and I used the same approach in London.

But while the strategy was supposed to give me a better chance of winning a gold medal, it was also a massive risk because the schedule was so demanding. Fortunately, as the Games got nearer my training was going quite well. As the Olympics exploded into life in China, I began to feel quietly confident. I was glued to the TV whenever I wasn't training. The opening ceremony was such an awesome display of power, I will never forget it. And then watching Usain Bolt take over the event, make it his own. That was amazing. His performance in the 100m final was from another planet – seeing him nearly running backwards through the line, waving to the crowd and breaking that world record. He is a phenomenal athlete. I remember a drug tester knocking on my door early one morning and I wasn't ready to pee so we sat there in my kitchen watching the live coverage and drinking tea. It was quite surreal.

Before the Olympics were over it was time to pack and head to China myself. The British team was supposed to be flying to a holding camp on the island of Macau but at the last minute it was changed to Hong Kong because the track was supposed to be better for wheelchair racers. But we still had to go to Beijing and then get a connection down to Hong Kong and back. Because of my fear of flying I asked if I could cut out the extra flight and go straight to Beijing. I knew my stress levels would go through the roof and I might get ill again. They said they would look into it. But it turned out the facilities in Beijing weren't open until much later and there would be no back-up or medical staff around to help me. So I had to go to Hong Kong. Not because they made me – there was no alternative.

On the flight from London, UKA refused to tell me which airline was handling the connection from Beijing. I was dreading it so much and they probably knew I would get stressed out. When I found out it was an airline called Dragon Air I just went mad. 'Who are Dragon Air?' I thought.

I was sitting on the plane at Hong Kong listening to the brakes all squeaking and the engines cranking up, thinking, I have got another three and a half hours of this. When we took off I swapped with a teammate who had a whole row to himself. I tried to pull myself together and eventually we arrived at the camp. It was such a relief. I had got myself so worked up about it and I felt slightly ridiculous. But I just couldn't help it. It is just the way I am.

Hong Kong at that time of year is extremely hot. The humidity is also terribly high. Add to that the problems I had adapting to the time difference and you had a recipe for disaster. Even after we got to Beijing, three weeks into the trip, I was still having problems. I couldn't sleep so I took some sleeping pills. That really worried me. Would they affect my training?

When we got to Beijing I found a city transformed from the place I had left in May. Blue skies and sunshine. No cars on the road, loads of people on bikes. Where had the smog gone? It was amazing. The Olympic village was one of the best I had ever seen. Everything was built on such a massive scale and was so well organised. It was really impressive.

My worries about the attitudes of the Chinese people hadn't gone away completely. On the face of it they seemed to be saying and doing all the right things – but then, there was a lot at stake for them. The whole world was watching them to see how they staged the Olympics and Paralympics. All I know is that the stadiums went on to be packed and that as athletes we only ever encountered people being nice and helpful. The question is whether the promises made during the Beijing Paralympics will be kept in ten years' time. If it genuinely leads to a change in the way disabled people are treated then that will have been a great achievement. I guess it's just too soon to judge.

By the time I arrived in China I had no time to worry about politics or equality issues. Because despite my best intentions to manage my illness and my training the final run-in to the Games in Beijing was going badly.

A day or two before it all started I was starting to feel a little bit rough so I dropped out of going to the opening ceremony. It was a shame as I wanted to be there to see it first-hand. After the Olympic ceremony the expectations were really high. But I couldn't take any chances. I was already taking loads of vitamin C to boost my immune system, but the day after the ceremony I woke up feeling less than great. I had a sore throat, I felt cold. 'Here we go,' I thought. I knew I had just done a week too much of training and now I was ill again. The glandular fever was always there. If ever I was next to someone with a cold, I would get it. Then it would become a chest infection. I just started fearing the worst. A lot of people thought it was all in my head and I was just panicking. But I knew how I felt.

To be fair, I could understand why UKA and some of the other coaches might have thought it was a psychological thing. There was undoubtedly a pattern in my behaviour before big championships. I always thought I was going to get ill, even before I got glandular fever. I wasn't a very positive person. Jenny always had to build me up. I am insecure about everything.

In the call room or on the warm-up track just before races, I make sure I don't show any of my opponents my fears and insecurities. The image I project is one of calmness and serenity. I am just in the zone. I don't like music or anything like that. I just sit there. I like watching the other athletes. All flapping around. Getting their wheelchairs ready, checking their tyres, tweaking their gloves. I always make sure I have done all that. I just sit there and watch and play mind games. I want to look as relaxed as possible.

I know the truth, though. Inside I am really nervous. I can't wait to race and get it out the way. I want to get to the finish. Get it over. I enjoy a race if it's going well, if I feel comfortable. But most races I want to be over before they have started.

When I met my girlfriend Emily she spotted the lack of confidence straight away. I came to accept it was a pattern that I had to confront. But it took Emily to break the cycle. She has changed me. She has made me a lot more positive about things and brought me a lot of confidence.

But back in Beijing I genuinely had something to worry about. In my first final, the 5,000m, the doctors had to give me Sudafed to clear my nose. It's on the banned drugs list now, but I had to take something to get to the start line. I couldn't even feel my body when the gun went off. I was completely out of it for the last three or four laps. Somehow

I got a bronze. It was a miracle, but everyone outside the team was asking how I hadn't won. After all, I had set the world record in the distance a year earlier. But I hadn't told any of the media or anyone outside the team doctors and coaches that I was ill before the race.

After that final I got worse. I went to the doctor and he did some tests and saw my iron count was really low. He said I shouldn't even be out of bed. He gave me an iron shot and it did make me feel a little bit better but I wasn't counting on anything. The doctor said it could take three months to have a real impact. But after a couple of days I felt a change. The jab had worked.

Up next was the 800m. I had come through the heats and the semi-final OK and now I felt ready to have a crack at my first gold. But it was to be one of the most controversial races of my career.

I remember going down to the start line – my main rivals, Kurt Fearnley and Marcel Hug, were there. After the lane draw I knew I had lane five and Kurt had lane seven. I was most worried about him because I knew he was pushing really strong.

So we were sitting in the call room and Kurt said to me, 'What number have they put on my helmet?'

'Two,' I said.

'But I am in lane seven or, at least I am supposed to be,' he replied. 'Well, that's better than seven, isn't it?'

Of course it is. He knew full well it was. To explain briefly, the best start lane for the 800m is number one.

That's because for the first 100 metres you have to go in a straight line and then cut across into a bunch. Setting your chair up to steer from a wide lane like number seven or eight is really hard and you can quickly lose an advantage in a race that is only two laps of the track. In short, the wider out you are, the harder life becomes.

'You lucky bastard, you've got a better lane,' I said.

I honestly thought he might flag it up and tell the officials. But not once did he complain about the mistake. He kept his mouth shut. He never went to the line judge or the referee. The officials didn't flag it up either. And you could see they were questioning it too. No one said anything. They had a big opportunity to do it. I was pretty certain Kurt was thinking that if he didn't win then he would get a rerun. A second chance. It was dirty tactics. Up in the stands the Australian Federation were going mad that he was in the wrong lane, but apparently that message never got through to trackside. They had a good ten minutes to flag it up, but nothing happened.

We lined up, started, and I was off and away in a good position. It came to the final lap and Kurt got boxed in. He couldn't get out. I could see he was trying but he couldn't catch me. I crossed the line. I had won my first Paralympic gold medal. I just thought, 'I've done it now.' That's all I wanted – one gold medal. My strategy of doing lots of events had paid off.

My mind raced straight back to Sydney and that devastating feeling of watching Tanni and others winning and me feeling lost, like I had wasted my life and let my country down. I was ecstatic. It was the best feeling I had ever experienced. I wrapped myself in the Union flag and savoured every moment of my victory lap. Most of the Chinese had left the stadium and there were no family or friends to see my moment of triumph. Not even Jenny, who was watching at home on the TV. But it still tasted so sweet. After everything I had been through – the drugs, the break-up, the illness. I was still a winner.

But then as I got back to the changing rooms I saw the team manager, Tim Jones. He didn't look very happy. I knew something was up. He told me there had been a protest.

'A what?' I shouted. 'What for? I didn't come out of my lane.'

And then I realised what had happened. There had been a complaint from the Australian team about Kurt's lane.

At that point I completely lost the plot. The IPC didn't even go to the referee or any other country. They took Australia's word for it and then they were standing there telling me I might have to have a rerun. I told them, 'I will not have a rerun. That is my gold medal. I won that fair and square.'

Underneath the stadium I was like a volcano erupting. I picked up whatever I could find and hurled it at the walls. I screamed wildly, shouting 'fuck this' and 'fuck that'. It must have been a terrifying sight. But I felt so robbed. I had been ill all week. And now they were threatening to take it all away from me. Besides, I had a busy schedule. When

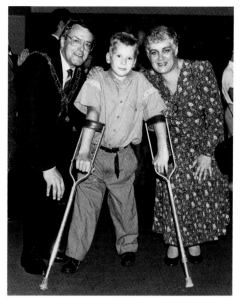

One of my first school pictures.

Out and about, with the Mayor of Kingston (left).

At school again, here aged eleven or twelve.

LEFT Norman Lamont, former MP for Kingston upon Thames, came down to see us training at Kingston track.

RIGHT With Steve Cram (right), who was one of the world's top middle-distance runners during the 1980s, after I completed the London mini-marathon.

Training in the evening at Kingston track.

LEFT Jacqueline Bullen, Benjamin Harwood, Stacey Burns, Heather Hodge and Jenny Archer (my incredible coach) carried the Paralympic flame on the torch relay leg between the City of Westminster and Lambeth.

RIGHT Ronie on her ninth birthday.

Daddy's girl, Tilly.

With my fiancée Emily at a friend's wedding.

Fireworks light up the Olympic Stadium in London during the opening ceremony of the Paralympic Games.

A moment of glory: celebrating my 800m win.

Rounding a bend in the Paralympic marathon.

On the final lap of the marathon, just eight miles from the finish line.

A picture I will always treasure: Mason in his GB shorts, me holding a union flag above our heads.

Two days after the marathon, my family and friends organised a surprise party I will never forget.

LEFT Being made a CBE by the Princess Royal at Buckingham Palace, March 2013.

RIGHT I was deeply honoured to receive a CBE. After all, I am only doing something I love. With my fiancée Emily and daughter Ronie.

LEFT With Tatyana McFadden (USA), Shelly Woods (GBR) and Hiroyuki Yamamoto (JPN) during a press photo shoot ahead of the London Marathon, April 2013.

RIGHT Enjoying a day out at the Royal Ascot, June 2013.

A special 1-Mile event back in the Olympic stadium, July 2013. The crowd numbered 60,000 – happy memories!

ABOVE Out in front in the Mile during day three of the Sainsbury's Anniversary Games.

LEFT With Mason and Ronie after winning the Mile.

would I get the chance to have a rerun? How are you going to fit in another 800m?

I was supposed to get my medal that night but it was only when I got to doping that I was told the presentation wasn't going to happen, that there could be another race.

Then I saw Kurt. He was also waiting in doping. I had it out with him.

I accused his lot of cheating. 'Where's the sportsmanship?' I asked him.

'You would have done the same thing,' he said.

But I wouldn't. I had a sense of right and wrong. A sense of fairness. And this was not fair. Kurt should have known what lane he was supposed to be in, we had discussed it before the race.

We very nearly came to blows. I told the Great Britain team doctor I was going back to the village. But they kept me at the track for ages as Tim Jones was trying to sort it out. The IPC just didn't listen – they just took the Australian team's word. And they call us whinging Poms, but they are the worst losers in the world. I am sorry to say it but I just felt so angry.

Kurt and I had been good friends. We had trained together a year earlier in Portugal. We would have a laugh and have a beer together after races. But all that went instantly. This was my first gold and he was threatening to take it away from me. If he had won I wouldn't have protested. He tried to claim I would have. But I wouldn't have done that.

I remember when I got back to the food hall very late, I could see Pete Wyman was there nearly crying. At that stage the British athletics team hadn't won a gold. There was a lot of pressure on my shoulders. I had been watching the rest of the team in other events on the TV praying for them to win a medal before I did so I didn't have to be the first. There had been a lot of focus on me.

It was very late when I called my mum back home. I was in tears. I told her this wasn't racing. This wasn't what the Paralympics should be about. I said I was coming home and told Tim Jones to book me a flight.

To try and help me come to terms with everything the team doctors and coaches suggested I go and see the British Paralympic Association's sports psychologist. He asked me, 'At this precise moment what would you do if you saw Kurt?'

'Probably strangle him to death,' I said. I was just being honest. If he had come into the room I would have lost it. I had worked so hard to get to this point and then it had been taken away from me by some whinging idiot.

He didn't know how to take that. At that precise moment I didn't want to talk to anyone. I needed to get out of that conversation and out of that room and think for myself. So I just left.

It was now two or three in the morning, and I called Jenny. She tried to tell me to stay and focus on the 1,500m. To prove to people I could do it. I wish Jenny had been out there in Beijing. Someone who loved me. Putting their arm around me and picking up the pieces. I really needed her at the time of the dispute with the Australians. But she wasn't able to get fully accredited as a member of the British coaching team in China. Places were limited and there was only so much money to go around. She really deserved to be accredited, but because she was only coaching me, it wasn't possible. I had to make do with her on the end of the phone.

I eventually went to bed but I didn't get much sleep that night. I was so angry.

At 11.30 the next morning Pete Wyman knocked on my door. He slumped on the floor and said, 'I've just received this letter from the Australian Federation and Kurt.'

'Read it to me.' I could see he was crying.

Kurt had apologised. He went on, 'Dave is a great athlete, I don't want him to have his medal taken away from him.'

He had forced the Australian Federation to withdraw the protest.

But when I got my medal the next day it just didn't feel special. I didn't want to shake Kurt's hand on the podium even though, in the end, he had done the right thing. Maybe I was old school and had different attitudes. But Kurt had been my friend. I don't trust anyone when I race any more. It killed me. To win my first Paralympic gold medal and not be able to really appreciate it.

It should have been really special for me, that moment. Because the athletics team were doing so badly I should have felt electric when I won. The pressure was off. I had done it and the country had something to be proud of. But on the podium I just felt empty.

I have actually tried over the years not to dwell too much on that race, which is really sad. I just want to try and forget about it.

That night, after the medal ceremony, I got back to the village, had a bit of food and then went to bed. I just kept looking at the medal. It was a great big thing with that green jade flash running through it. It was really beautiful. But for me it was tainted. It had been spoiled. I opened the drawer by my bed and put it in before closing it and locking it. I didn't do what some athletes do and sleep with it under their pillow or whatever. In the morning I didn't even take it out. I had to plan for the 1,500m and I had to mentally prepare for the next race.

I had learned from bitter experience in my early championships that you can't allow yourself to get carried away and get too excited. You have to get back to normal. Because I was still struggling with fitness, I was trying to be as chilled as possible and to conserve my energy. The Beijing Games was becoming a major battle against my body and my mind.

By the time the heats of the 1,500m arrived the next morning I was feeling a lot better. The medication was working. Plus the Red Bull, two or three cans a day just to keep going.

The heat went really well. I wanted that 1,500m more than anything. I didn't care about the time in the heat. Just get through. Shut everything out, Dave. Go through the motions. I felt good.

Then Kurt did a really fast time in his heat. The fact that Kurt was looking so good just made me even more determined to show I could beat him, this time without any doubts or distractions. But he was at his best in Beijing over 1,500m.

The rain fell heavily during the warm-up. But that didn't worry me one bit. I am normally pretty comfortable in the rain and when we started the track was still wet. It didn't dry out as quickly as I expected and was still quite greasy. I shot off real fast. Like a rocket. And on the first 100 metres I hit quite good speeds. Then I hit the bend and the whole back end of my chair skidded away from underneath me. The tyres just didn't seem to be gripping as they should have done. Then, with two laps to go I got boxed in by Marcel Hug. I was stuck. I wouldn't normally be in that position. I would normally race away and get out of trouble. But because it was wet, I was holding back. I knew as the finish got closer the pace was going to go up and when that happened there was going to be some kind of crash.

The last lap approached. I just couldn't get out. Marcel was getting closer and closer. We were knocking elbows now. I needed to get out. If I didn't, the race was over. I couldn't wait. If there was a crash I was screwed. Others wouldn't have let me out. He wouldn't have let me out. It's not that Marcel's a soft touch but maybe he had respect for me. Maybe he just didn't want to crash.

Our wheels were almost touching and if that happened that would be it. We were both going to end up in a heap. It was so tense. I was using so much energy on concentration, watching always, trying to weigh up when to go. I am quite good at moving my chair around, I can flick my hips and change direction instantly. I sit quite high so I am nimble enough to do that. Then all of a sudden Marcel sat up. It might have been no more than five seconds but the pace dropped, and that was all I needed. I switched direction and I was out. On the inside the pack was getting closer and closer. The crash was still coming.

And then it happened – total wipe-out. The whole field had pretty much been taken down by the most spectacular crash. It was perfect. Now all I had to do was pick up the pace into the last bend. The only challenger left was the Thai athlete Prawat Wahoram. But I knew I could beat him, that my top-end speeds were so much faster than his. So I just charged away, leaving the devastation behind me. And when I crossed the line it was the best feeling in the world.

I didn't care about how the race had gone and the crash. That's racing. I have been wiped out before. That's the way it goes. But after what happened with the 800m and the protest there was still a doubt in my mind – I wondered if it might happen all over again because of that crash. Someone else might try and take my gold away from me. So while I was celebrating I was also nervous that some other drama might lie ahead of me. The officials aren't supposed to order a rerun unless the crash happens in the first 200 metres but in the women's race the night before there had been a crash halfway through and it was run again next day, so what had happened there was in my mind. It was the first thing I asked after the race when I got off the track: was there a protest?

But this time there was no controversy, no screaming rows and sleepless nights. Just a feeling of satisfaction and joy. I had overachieved. Two golds and a bronze and I still had the 400m to go, although I knew at that stage there was no way I could do a marathon. Mentally I had pulled out of that race.

You have to give a lot of credit to Kurt for getting up from that crash and winning bronze, as he was 50 or 60 metres behind me. I didn't tell him that after the race, though. I still couldn't look him in the eye.

By the time I was on the podium with him receiving my medal and listening to 'God Save the Queen', the Bird's Nest was virtually empty. The minute the Chinese knew there was no home athlete involved, they went. I didn't care. I felt myself welling up when the national anthem was played. After everything that had gone on it was very emotional. I was tired, emotionally drained. But I was happy. Suddenly it all felt worth it. All those years of hard work. My feeling about the 1,500m medal was totally different to the 800m. I couldn't stop looking at it. I still put the new one into the drawer with the 800m one and locked it away in there with my socks and my pants. I only took it out to take a picture with it to send to my friend. But this one felt really special.

After that, whatever happened in the 400m didn't really matter. It was my favourite event, but China had a genuine local hero to cheer on in Zhang Lixin. He was absolutely flying, way ahead of me in terms of the times he was doing in qualifying. My only chance of beating him was if it rained, because I knew he was crap in the wet. I had raced him in May at the Paralympic World Cup and I beat him by 20 metres.

But here in Beijing he completely destroyed me, winning the 400m by an incredible margin of 60 metres. In those short few months he had become a totally different athlete. And I was moving pretty fast myself, clocking a time which was faster than my old world record for the distance. The speeds he was hitting were just frightening. I have since watched the race back in slow motion and he was putting such pressure down that he was deflating his front tyre. That was the first time I had been beaten in a 400m for three years.

It gave me a good taster of the power of a home crowd behind you. In Beijing, whenever a Chinese athlete was involved the atmosphere in the Bird's Nest was deafening. It made me want to fast-forward four years to London and my moment in my home town.

Despite the defeat by Lixin I was more than satisfied with my return in Beijing. OK, so maybe the media expected me to win five golds. But I knew what I had been through in the run-up to the Games. I was still ill and yet I had delivered. My golds were the only ones won by the athletics team, which was a massive disappointment.

Overall the Chinese medal tally was scary: 211, with 89 golds, was just off the scale. But when you look at the sheer population of that country you know it is impossible for a country like Great Britain to compete. With the exception of the athletics team, it had been a fantastic Games for Paralympics GB, though. We won 102 medals and finished second in the medal table behind the Chinese. It was the moment we really announced our arrival as a Paralympic force.

We had even beaten the Americans into third place. But then America's attitude to the Paralympics is strange. I often feel sorry for the American athletes because they have real talent and yet they get hardly any coverage in the media for the Paralympics, even though in the big city marathons you are treated like a superstar. It's bizarre and I think the country should do more to help their disabled athletes. It is a strange contradiction that a country like China should take the Paralympics more seriously than a country like America. I hope they step up in the future.

As for the rest of my Games, I pulled out of the marathon straight after the 400m. The team officials understood. They were expecting it. I just didn't have enough energy. Now it was done I could relax.

Having missed the opening ceremony I was determined to enjoy the closing party. We had a few beers before going over to the stadium for one last time. I just felt so relieved it was over. I had been away for a month and a bit and I couldn't wait to get on that flight and go home – which was obviously a bit strange for me.

After the ceremony Boris Johnson threw a brilliant party for the team at one of the Beijing hotels. Free beers, free food. He gave a speech and had a chat to me and some of the other athletes. He told me I would make London proud in four years' time. We had never had this sort of celebration or recognition before. Much of this was being driven by the need to make a success of the London Paralympics: from the very beginning the London organising committee had made it clear that they wanted to treat the Paralympics as an equal partner to the Olympics. I knew this would lead to a step change in the way we were treated and viewed. And on that heady night in Beijing I felt the start of something really special, a shift in attitudes. For the first time it felt like we were being taken seriously.

I didn't want that night to end. I recruited Pete Wyman as my drinking partner and, along with a few other members of the squad, we headed to the BBC party. I was still up as dawn approached. The only problem was, we had to be ready to leave for the airport for our flight home at 6.15 a.m. And now the others had all left me and I was still lost somewhere in the city. I jumped into a cab.

Pete Wyman rang me, asking, 'Where are you?'

'I don't really know, Pete,' I said. 'In a taxi somewhere.'

I told the driver, 'Take me to the Olympic village. And fast.'

He had no idea what I was saying. So he stopped and asked some other people at various hotels. Blank looks. So he tried again. Same shoulder shrugs. This seemed to go on for ages. Back at the village someone was in my room packing my bags for me.

I phoned Pete again.

'I still don't know where I am,' I told him.

Now they were getting a bit worried. Pete went to Tim Jones, who was our team manager, and broke the news. Tim said, 'He is old enough and brave enough. If he can't get back here just meet us at the airport.' He was absolute class, so calm.

Meanwhile I was still going round and round in circles. Totally lost. Then, somehow in my drunken state, I remembered I had my accreditation on, so I looked down and found the Chinese symbol for Olympic village. I showed it to the driver. He understood and thankfully I was only three or four miles away. What an entrance I made that morning. What a state I must have looked. I remember coming in through the barriers, round to the GB team's apartment blocks, and everyone was there. Waiting. They all had their official kit on. Everyone was cheering and clapping. I dashed up to my room, no time to change. I was still wearing my parade kit from the closing ceremony. It was only thanks to one of the team's assistants that I even had my bags ready to go. I jumped on the coach and took a long, deep breath. At the airport I was just so happy to see that plane with the gold wing tips and nose. Then I found out the best news of all. All gold-medal winners had been allocated a seat in business class. What a lucky touch.

And then it got even better. At first I was allocated a

window seat, which is difficult for wheelchair users as they have to clamber over someone else to get to the toilet. They looked into moving me but said there were no available seats as all the aisle spaces in business were already taken by people with wheelchairs. I was about to settle down when suddenly one of the stewardesses approached me and told me they had found a seat and that they were going to move me. I thought I might be heading to the back of the plane but instead we went forwards. Right to the front of the plane. And I mean the very front. Seat number one. Sebastian Coe, who was on the same flight home as us, had agreed to swap it with me. I couldn't thank him enough. He has been a great ambassador for the Paralympics.

Once the plane took off, I was out like a light. I must have slept the whole way home. I was so hungover. When we landed at Terminal 5 we were given an amazing reception. At that time the building work was still going on and all the construction workers were cheering as we taxied to the gate. That's when I started to realise that we were being recognised, that things were starting to change for us Paralympians. Mind you, because of a mix-up with my luggage I missed a photo call with the Prime Minister, Gordon Brown. I didn't mind that too much – I was so tired I just wanted to see my family.

When I came through arrivals my mum was there to meet me with Ronie. I hadn't expected that. I cried when I saw them. I told them I was mentally drained and I felt shocking. I had been out all night, I hadn't showered, I'd been ten hours on a plane, my hair was everywhere. I looked a mess and I just wanted to get home. Then my mum told me there was a big reception waiting for me back on Roundshaw. I didn't want to do it at the time but when I got to the Phoenix Centre on the estate there was this huge mob of people and a big banner congratulating me. I said a few words. I don't remember what. It just came out. And then there were all these kids just wanting to see and touch my medals. Seeing how those kids reacted to the medals was really special. Maybe that would keep them off the streets and stop them making the same mistakes that I made all those years back.

Suddenly the medals felt even more precious. Until you show them off you don't know the impact. After a couple of days of catching up with friends and getting some sleep I went to see Jenny. It was quite emotional and she was crying. She always has a tear in her eye when I do well. For her, this was the culmination of a life's work. But as she contemplated what we had done in China she also had her mind on the next challenge. Beijing was just the beginning. London was coming.

CHAPTER 8

SETTLING DOWN

I hadn't had much luck with relationships. After the split from Kaylie I had become deeply distrustful of women. Over time those feelings had eased but I was still very cautious. I didn't want to get hurt again. When I came back from Beijing I had a few flings but nothing serious. Then I met Emily Thorne.

It was May 2009 and I was taking it pretty easy on the training front. I was just having a drink in my local when I saw her. She was just popping out for a fag and I said hello. I knew who she was but we hadn't really spoken before. She didn't live on the estate, but she was still local. I stopped her in the doorway and talked to her for a bit. Then, either later that night or the day after, we connected through Facebook and started to chat.

From there, things moved pretty fast. I took her to the cinema to see the Dan Brown sequel to *The Da Vinci Code*, *Angels and Demons*. She didn't like it very much but the film was irrelevant. It was the start of something really special.

At first I was slightly worried Emily was a bit young – I was twenty-nine and she was nineteen. But she didn't talk or act like someone immature. She wasn't young in the head – she probably acted older than me sometimes. She was like no one else I have ever been with. She knew I was into wheelchair athletics, but she didn't really know what I had done, and had no idea that I'd won gold medals in Beijing or anything like that. When she came to understand, it didn't make any difference. I liked that about her. From the very start, really, I knew she was the one. You just get that feeling, don't you? You can't explain it. She is just so genuine and caring, a decent person to talk to. She tells me now that in the early days when we had just started going out all I used to talk about was my racing. I must have been quite boring and I guess I'm lucky she's still here. I just talked about racing and training. But it's that honesty that has changed me as a person. It's made me better as a racer. I can now switch off and try to talk about other things.

After about a month we started talking seriously about moving in together. She had left school with good grades and was working in the local branch of NatWest. She was renting her own flat but because I was on my own in the house she used to stay over a lot. The first time she stayed, I dropped her back at her house at 6 a.m. because I had to go to training. It gave her a taste of what was to come, but she took it well.

Given my past experiences I wondered whether things were going too quickly, whether I was stepping in too fast. But I had learned from my mistakes. If she went out I wouldn't get paranoid. I believed in her. I knew she wasn't going to betray me and I think that's why I instantly fell in love with her and knew that we'd be together for a long time.

Right from the start Emily knew I had a daughter from a previous relationship but she never expressed any concern about my past suddenly becoming part of her present. I still didn't rush things; I wanted to wait to make sure I knew where it was headed first. But when the time came the two of them hit it off straight away.

A couple of months after we got together, I went off to Ibiza for a lads holiday. I had never had the chance to do that before. I'd booked it before I met Emily and hadn't expected to be in a serious relationship. In the end I spent most of my time texting or calling her. But my ten days there, going to the clubs, staying up through the night, chilling on the beach, were still amazing. Obviously drugs are everywhere in Ibiza, in all the clubs and bars. But it never crossed my mind. I would just have a few beers and have a laugh and that was it. I had left those days behind long ago.

That holiday summed up the year after Beijing. 2008 had been brilliant – in the end. But it had been a major struggle, what with the illness and everything else going on at home. After all that I was determined to take it easy for a few months. I was still training and racing but the golden glow of the Games soon faded. I did get a bit of extra funding from UK Athletics but the race fees and the sponsorships didn't really change. There was a bit more recognition and I would be announced at meetings as the double gold medallist but I was hardly a superstar. It didn't bother me. I had got used to it and didn't have high expectations. I just did my own thing. I raced and trained and I didn't worry about recognition or money.

Later that year, Emily got pregnant. It was a total shock: completely unplanned and totally unexpected. It was so early on in our relationship. But it didn't seem to matter that we had only been together a few months. I was happy and so was Emily. We were ready.

That's why it was so hard to take when Emily miscarried. A couple of weeks before the twelve-week scan Emily suddenly started saying that she just didn't feel pregnant any more. I kept telling her it would all be OK. But when she had the scan, we were told there was no heartbeat. They couldn't see anything.

Instantly Emily's face changed colour. She was in total shock. I didn't know what to do. It was so, so hard because you have such high expectations and for her it was even worse. The hospital told us the baby had stopped growing at around six weeks.

Because it was so early in the pregnancy, we hadn't told many people. My mum knew, though, so when we got back home I told her the news. In floods of tears I explained how the baby had stopped developing, that there wasn't going to be a baby. The worst thing about the whole experience was that Emily was still carrying the baby. We had to go back home with it inside her. It absolutely killed her, knowing this little thing wouldn't grow any more. Even worse – she would have to go back a few days later and have an abortion. I did my best to comfort her but she was crying a lot. The whole experience made us inseparable.

When it was time to take her for the dreaded abortion, we found ourselves sitting in a waiting room where 90 per cent of the women obviously didn't want their children. All Emily could think about was the fact that she wanted her baby and yet all these other women were giving it all away. It broke our hearts.

I tried to make Emily feel better by telling her that perhaps there had been something wrong with the baby and this was nature's way of dealing with it. Maybe it wasn't a healthy egg. I asked her, 'I know I'm disabled, but could you live with a disabled child?'

I knew I couldn't. It would destroy me because I know what I went through. It's slightly different for me because I'm more able than most. But because I was brought up disabled, I wouldn't want a child to be brought up in the same situation as me. This sounds incredibly cold and heartless but I would probably consider an abortion if I knew for sure that a child of mine would be disabled – because of my own experience. You don't know how disabled they're going to be. My mum and dad didn't even know. They didn't have a choice. I'm so happy and blessed that my children can run around and do the things I could never do. It makes me smile when I see Mason running around the sitting room, jumping on the sofa, because I could never do those things. When I come home and he comes running towards me, it makes my day.

I know my experience would help a disabled child to come to terms with whatever problems and challenges they had, but I always just prayed that it would never happen to my kids.

Maybe in the future, science and medical care will advance to the point where they can correct disabilities like mine. It is already possible for people who have had an accident to undergo therapy which might help them walk again. If you have known what it is like to walk and then you lose it, it's obvious you would want to get that back. But it's not as obvious for people like me as you might imagine. How do you learn to do something you have never known? And what might the people close to you think? Would it change the way they see you? Personally, if someone said they could wave a magic wand and give me the power to move my legs then I probably would. But it wouldn't be easy to come to terms with something like that, as idealistic as it sounds.

It took Emily a long time to come round to thinking that it wasn't meant to be. But a year later she was pregnant with Mason. This time she went for early scans – no one was going to take any chances. Inevitably, she was so scared of losing that baby, petrified of every single pain or twinge that she felt. We were always up the hospital. All I could do was tell her that everything was going to be fine. And just hope.

Mason was born on 1 August 2011. After everything we had been through it was just such an enormous relief, the best feeling in the world. We knew we were having a boy, and for me that was extra special. He came a month early because by that stage Emily was so big. He was seven pounds and three ounces – and that was with four weeks to go. Imagine how big he might have been if Emily had gone full term.

Even though none of the scans had raised any issues or concerns, I still had my doubts. When the midwife handed him to me, I immediately checked he had all his fingers and toes. Made sure his legs were working. But he was fine. So alert, his little eyes already scanning the room.

For Emily it had been a painful experience. Although the labour was relatively short – seven hours – she had to stay in hospital. It was nothing serious, just a few stitches and a couple of nights of observation. She was so worried about someone coming and swapping Mason for another baby that she was terrified of going to the toilet.

I was so proud of my new little boy. And when he started to smile and recognise me as his daddy, it gave me such a lift. Whenever I came back from a bad training session or I was hurting, I would instantly forget all about it. It made me stronger as a person. Training and competing just became my day job. It was different to how it had been with Ronie – I was only twenty-four when she came along. I was young and naive then, and this time I wanted to be more involved. Even though Mason came a year before

London, I was never worried about him being a distraction because I had always wanted a family. Life comes first and, besides, he actually helped me with training. He gave me a greater drive and sense of purpose. Now I wasn't only doing this for me, I was doing it for Emily and my family. A better future for all of us.

CHAPTER 9

THE ENEMY WITHIN

Drive a few miles north of the Olympic Park at Stratford and you come to the Lee Valley, a sprawling stretch of London which the rest of the city seems to have forgotten. Although it extends into the Essex and Hertfordshire countryside, much of it is an ugly mix of industrial estates, train lines and electricity pylons. A fortune has been spent on it in recent years to try and redevelop it and smarten it up. It's there, in a bit of the park just outside Edmonton, that you will find the Lee Valley Athletics Centre, the nerve centre of the sport in Great Britain.

In the run-up to London 2012 the head coaches from UK Athletics ordered all contenders for the Olympic and Paralympic squads to base themselves there. I totally understood why. It had cost about £15 million to build and was an impressive place, with fantastic facilities. But for me, it was a total waste of time. I couldn't wait to get away.

It was November 2010: just under two years to go to the Games. I had just won the New York Marathon, probably my biggest achievement since Beijing. Until then I had been overweight and struggling. Unbelievable as it might sound with a home Olympics and Paralympics just around the corner, I just couldn't get motivated. Whenever I got in my chair that summer I felt uncomfortable. I was way above my optimum weight of 58 kilos. I don't know if it was because I was bursting at the seams or if there was a problem with my chair set-up but I had to put padding around everything to stop it hurting me when I raced. My legs would tingle whenever I stayed in my chair for a long time. I was beginning to worry.

When I look back at pictures from that period now, I think, 'How on earth did I push my chair?' My arms were all flabby and I look so out of shape. In races that year, it was always a struggle just to stay in contention. But it can't have been that bad as I was always there or thereabouts. I knew at that point that as long as I got my head down and worked hard I would be able to get back to my best.

New York was the moment which really announced my return to form. I had to really train hard through the late summer and autumn but by November I felt much happier. I had got myself a new chair and I set off with Emily in confident mood. It was the first time we had been to New York together and it was great to have her with me. I had done most of the hard yards by the time we landed so I only had to do light training sessions once I got to New York. We were staying in a lovely hotel in Manhattan and after break-fast I would get in my race chair and push up to Central

Park for a gentle work-out. I used to get a few funny looks from New Yorkers as they made their way to work, but I loved the place. After training I would head back and shower and change before spending the rest of the day with Emily, shopping or taking in the sights. It felt like a holiday.

I had to snap out of my chilled-out mood when it came to race day. This was no city break. It was really hard going and I had to fight all the way to the end to beat Japan's Masazumi Soejima in a sprint finish. My arms were hurting so much, because I went for it too early. In the end I was hitting the push rims on my wheels so hard I couldn't really feel anything. Somehow, I held on.

As I crossed the line, Emily was the first person I saw. I headed straight for her and she gave me a massive cuddle. It was the first time she had been at a big event with me so to have her there when I won was magical, really special. Winning New York had always been one of my ambitions. But because it always came at the end of a busy track season, it often felt like one race too far. This year was the perfect moment and it gave me such a big lift.

Sadly, things turned sour quite quickly. After returning from America I was making the long journey to north-east London to Lee Valley two or three times a week for training. The World Championships in New Zealand were coming up in January and I needed to maintain my fitness and build up my strength. Lee Valley is undoubtedly a world-class facility and the physios and strength and conditioning coaches there are some of the best in the business.

But I didn't get treated like a world-class athlete. The staff there seemed to spend all their time focusing on the able-bodied athletes and us Paralympians were treated like second-class citizens. Sometimes they would forget that I was even turning up.

I was supposed to get one-on-one attention from one of the strength and conditioning coaches or the physios but it never seemed to work out that way. They were always popping to see me for a few minutes here and there before going back to see the able-bodied athletes. They weren't like Jenny and they weren't following her instructions. I had never worked with them before and they didn't know me, or my body, well enough. That's why I got injured.

Because of the distances involved, UKA agreed that I didn't have to drive across London to Lee Valley every day. So instead I split my time between there and my old routine of training on the roads of Richmond Park and on the track at St Mary's University College in Twickenham. But UKA were overseeing everything and they had me on weight-training programmes when I was working out on my own. One of them involved lifting up dumbbells straight in front of me. At first the coach told me to do a 6kg weight but I said there was no way my shoulders could cope with it. I privately overruled him and dropped it to a 4kg but it was still too much. During a session of lifting I suddenly felt a sharp, agonising pain in my right shoulder. To give you the full technical description, the bursa pad in my rotator cuff had been badly injured by the exercises. In simple terms: it was buggered. Just reaching up to use my front-door key would cause a sharp pain to shoot through my shoulder.

Now, I don't think the exercises were wrong. I just don't think they suited a disabled athlete or someone in a wheelchair. The coach thought they would help strengthen my shoulders but they didn't, they hurt them. As far as I am concerned this particular coach wasn't really suited to training Paralympians – he was more comfortable with training able-bodied athletes. It made me angry that I wasn't being given support tailored to me. After all, I was a double gold-medal winner and one of the biggest medal hopes for London. But that is just the way it is and I don't think it will change in my lifetime. We'll always be second best.

That's not to say there is any resentment or ill feeling between the able-bodied and the disabled athletes who compete for Great Britain. In fact, the opposite is true. I know a lot of the guys very well and they always talk to me as if we are all part of one big team. It's not their fault. I don't even blame the coach. It was the system.

At first, the shoulder didn't feel too bad but after a while I couldn't lift my arm above a certain degree. It was so sore and even doing little things like opening a drawer would make it click – it was really painful. Within a few weeks I was supposed to be flying out to New Zealand for the World Championships but my faith in the whole Lee Valley set-up had evaporated. That was when relations between me and UK Athletics started to fall apart.

After Beijing a lot of the really good people at UKA like Tim Jones, Pete Wyman and Kathryn Periac left. They were largely replaced by one man – Peter Eriksson. A Swede with a long and distinguished career in coaching, he had been hired a year earlier as the performance director for the Great Britain Paralympic athletics team. He was well known on the wheelchair racing circuit and had joined from Canada where he had a great track record, coaching gold-medal winners like Jeff Adams and Chantal Petitclerc. As an athlete he had been a speed skater but in coaching he moved into the mainstream world of athletics and then into disability sport.

With the tough-talking Dutchman Charles van Commenee overseeing the whole of the British athletics programme, it was Peter's job to make sure that Paralympic athletes like me were integrated with the Olympians in one big training and performance system. All the pressure on me to train at Lee Valley and to follow the guidance of the UKA coaches and physios came directly from Peter. But I am not the sort of person who responds well to that sort of pressure. I am an individual who likes to set my own agenda, and to work with my own coach and people I trust. From the start I knew we were going to clash.

New York was the first of a series of flashpoints which would almost derail my preparations and plans for London 2012. When Peter found out I'd injured my shoulder he assumed it was because of the New York Marathon. He hadn't wanted me to go in the first place. Jenny called him to explain it had happened in the gym but he claimed it was all the training I had done for New York. At that point Jenny's patience snapped. 'Dave told you he wanted to do New York,' she told him in a heated phone call. 'I'm his coach and I wanted him to do it and he won it. It was one of the best races I've seen him do in a long time.' After that Jenny told me there was silence at the other end of the line. That was one of the things I personally found frustrating with him. I found it hard to get any sense of what he was really thinking. He would probably say that was good leadership, a good way of motivating you. But I am not so sure. I never really knew where I stood with Peter.

The shoulder injury was starting to cause me real problems. It had brought a complete stop to all my training plans. And with time running out before the World Championships, UKA suggested I should resort to that last refuge all sportsmen and women must consider from time to time – the cortisone injection. Just before Christmas I went to see a specialist recommended to me by UKA at a clinic in St John's Wood. After giving me a shot of local anaesthetic, he then sank the enormous needle into my right shoulder.

The idea was to reduce the inflammation in my shoulder so I could train properly again. It wouldn't deal with any of the pain I was getting but it would take down the swelling. It worked straight away. After three days' rest I started training again and it felt great, totally back to normal. You can see why some athletes overuse it. You are only supposed to have two in your entire career but I am sure there are plenty of people who have taken more jabs than that just to keep going. That year I trained all the way through Christmas – except Christmas Day, of course. I am no Daley Thompson, who famously trained twice on 25 December. I just couldn't do that to the family. Now I've got kids it's even more important.

Despite the way the injection had worked I was still convinced by this stage that I wasn't going to go to New Zealand. I had missed nearly eight weeks of training and I felt I had no chance of winning any medals. I didn't want to go as an also-ran. Psychologically it would be too damaging so close to the London Games. I called Peter up to tell him the news. 'Look, David, you are going to the Worlds, and that's final,' he told me, in his usual blunt manner.

Now I completely lost it. I was shouting and swearing down the phone at him, trying to make him understand that I wasn't capable of winning. It was a real scene. He wouldn't back down and told me to think about it for a few days.

Then, on New Year's Eve, out of the blue, I got a call from UKA's sports psychologist, Sarah Cecil. That really got my back up. I don't think sports psychologists should be forced on people by governing bodies or coaches. It's something the athlete should decide to do. It made me deeply suspicious. I thought everything I said would end up going back to Peter. It was a complete waste of time.

As most people were getting ready to celebrate the New

Year that night I called Jenny to try to work out what to do. Ultimately it was Peter's call and he had already warned me I could lose my lottery funding (this wasn't the only time I heard that when I didn't fit into the UKA agenda). Jenny was getting so much flak from Peter about the way I was behaving. But she told me that night that she would stand by my decision, whatever it was.

On New Year's Day I rang Jenny again – I didn't want to speak to Peter – and told her my decision: 'OK, I will go. But don't count on anything. I will try to get as fit as I can in the time I have left.'

A day before we were due to leave, I called Peter and apologised for the way I had behaved. It hadn't been very professional to swear at him in the way I had. I told him I would see him at the airport. He just said, 'Okay, I'll see you there.' That was all he said. How could he be so unresponsive?

———

For a nervous flyer like me the prospect of a 24-hour flight to New Zealand was a nightmare. But I was so worried about all the training I had missed that I forgot a lot of my fears. I asked the medical staff if they could work out a way of getting me over the jet lag quickly, so that when we got to the pre-Championships training camp in Auckland I could start working on my fitness straight away. As the plane took off for the first leg of the trip to Los Angeles, we were all given melatonin and some vitamins. They worked a treat and when I woke up I wasn't groggy at all. In fact, I didn't have any jet lag until five or six days after we got there. It was exactly what I needed and it gave me a great advantage – I was able to get straight into my training.

Before I left Jenny had another word with Peter. She talked him through the programme she had set up for me and told him that she wanted him – and only him – to look after me. I think she wanted to see if he would try to adapt it or put his own stamp on it. When he came to look at it, I could see that he thought it wasn't going to work. But at that stage he had only ever come to see me train once and that was when he had just got the job in 2009. He didn't know anything about the intensity I put into my training sessions.

After the first couple of days in Auckland he could see it was working. I was getting fitter and fitter each day. By the end of the week my confidence was starting to grow. I was starting to feel like I might have a chance of actually winning something.

Suddenly the team psychologist Sarah Cecil was back. She came to my room in Auckland, sat on my floor and tried to start a conversation with me. I was having none of it. 'Can I help you?' I asked her, my surly tone impossible to miss.

She asked how I was feeling but I just didn't want to play ball. It just didn't feel right and all the time I was just thinking that she was going to feed whatever I told her back to Peter. I know these days modern sport is full of scientists, medics and motivational specialists but maybe I am just a bit old fashioned. I didn't trust the situation. Deep down I knew what I wanted to say: I was angry. And I was scared. Scared of coming home empty handed. Scared of piling even more pressure on my shoulders. Rightly or wrongly, I felt like I was the biggest name in the men's Paralympics team going into London. If I didn't win at the World Championships then I was putting myself up there to be shot at.

After a good week or so training in Auckland we moved from the North Island to the South and the beautiful host city of Christchurch. The World Championships had never been staged outside Europe before – never mind in the far-flung southern hemisphere. Even though my build-up had been pretty disastrous, it was exciting to be on the other side of the world competing at such a big event. The British team arrived in high spirits.

None of us could have expected what we would watch unfold on our TV screens just three weeks after we left. In the middle of February an enormous earthquake, measuring 6.3 on the Richter scale, tore through the city killing 185 people, destroying buildings and even ripping up the track on which we raced. Even when we were there in mid-January I felt what people told me were just minor tremors. To me, some of them felt quite powerful and left me feeling quite rough. One day I came out of the shower and I could see the building opposite actually moving. It was a really weird feeling but, although I felt a bit unsure, everyone reassured me that it was normal and there was never any talk of cancelling the championships. But I kept thinking, 'What if it happens when we're competing?' My heart goes out to all the people who were caught up in that tragedy. We were so lucky to get out when we did.

When it came to the racing, I saw Christchurch as a bit of a dry run for London. I targeted the four events I would race for in 2012 – the 800m, 1,500m, 5,000m and the marathon. It was madness, really, when you think about it. The cortisone injection was only masking the deeper problems with my shoulder. If I were to stand any chance then I had to get off to a winning start. I also knew I had to adapt my racing. I had to be much smarter about timing my attacks. In the past I had always panicked whenever one of the other big guns hit the front. Here I would have to be more intelligent and save my energy for when it really counted.

The 800m was first up. I just scraped through the heats but in the final I felt good. My nemesis, Marcel Hug, was leading with 120 metres to go, but as we came off the final bend I went for it. I came out of his slipstream and took him on. It was neck and neck down the home straight but somehow I found my Beijing speed and just pipped him on the line. I had kept enough in reserve to beat him. The win gave me such a lift – it was so unexpected that I thought I didn't have anything to lose now. In the 1,500m I played the same waiting game, sitting on Marcel's tail until the last bend and then going for the front. I could see by the look on his face when I glanced back that it ruined him. This time I won by a good chair's length.

With two golds already in the bag I approached the 5,000m with a bit more trepidation. I knew my lack of stamina wouldn't show up in the two middle-distance events but in the longer races I thought I might still struggle. Again, my waiting tactics paid off. I tried to conserve as much energy as possible, only using my pace and covering breaks when I really had to. I just stayed in touch and as we went into the last lap I was sat nicely on Prawat Wahoram's back wheel. With about 300 metres to go I upped the pace, taking the Thai athlete on, and hitting the front off the final bend. I raised my arms in jubilation as I crossed the line to claim my third gold of the Championships. I couldn't believe it. I went to New Zealand expecting – fearing – I would come away with nothing. But I got three golds, the same as in Assen in 2006. What was more satisfying this time was the way I had raced, conserving my energy and staying calm.

At that point I was already thinking the marathon might be a race too far. I only had a day and a half to recover and I was dreading the prospect of 26 miles. Fortunately, my mind was made up for me. Amazingly, the International Paralympic Committee forgot to apply for a licence to close the roads around Christchurch. It was absolutely unbelievable. The minute I heard there would be cars on the roads, I pulled out. It was embarrassing and dangerous. Would this have happened in an able-bodied World Championships? They had marshals but they couldn't guarantee athletes would be safe. In fact, when the race took place a car pulled off a drive as the wheelchair athletes were going past and nearly hit some of them.

Peter Eriksson had found out about all this the night before the marathon but didn't tell me until 5 a.m. on the day of the race. I was annoyed at the time because I could have gone out and celebrated with some of my teammates. But I was angrier at the IPC. Again, I felt they weren't running these events properly. The crowds in Christchurch were like those in Atlanta – hardly anyone turned up and it just wasn't promoted properly. I told the IPC their mistake had potentially cost me and Great Britain another medal. It was ridiculous. They knew when the Championships were happening. Why didn't they think to apply for a licence?

Despite that unsatisfactory ending, New Zealand had still been a brilliant World Championships for me. After we got back to London, I called Peter and sent him an email apologising for the way I had behaved before we left. I admitted I had been out of order but said I had been frightened. I thought we might start to get on a bit better. But things soon started to go downhill again.

After a couple of weeks of rest I was soon back training at Lee Valley. But it didn't take long before I was feeling like a second-class citizen again. It was so frustrating. I just wasn't getting the same treatment as the able-bodied athletes. I used to sit there and wonder if this was really happening. Am I not a world-class athlete? Have I not just won three gold medals at a World Championships? I really wanted to start working with a dedicated strength and conditioning coach, but I was being told I might have to wait until September. I couldn't understand it. There were loads of coaches in the gym but none of them could find the time to work with me for an hour. When I raised it with anyone at UKA they just brushed it off or denied it was even happening. But I knew what was going on. I tried to make it work and I had tried to draw a line under the row with Peter but now things just deteriorated. I lost all respect for him.

New York and New Zealand had strained our relationship to breaking point. Now the more familiar city of Birmingham would provide the setting for our third big disagreement. I had actually started the season quite well. My Christmas-time cortisone was still doing the business and I won the London Marathon for a fifth time in April. But by June my injection had worn off and my right shoulder was injured again. The doctors tried the same trick again, sending me for a second cortisone injection, and, this time, telling me to rest completely. The only thing on the horizon was a Diamond League event in Birmingham. With the doctor's advice ringing in my ears, I decided to pull out.

Next thing I know, Peter is on the phone to Jenny, asking if I can compete after all. She refused, explaining what the doctors had told me. To this day I still don't understand why he asked me to compete when he knew I was injured.

It really shook my confidence in him as a coach. It was definitely a new low point.

Maybe a lot of the problems with Peter stemmed from the fact that he didn't coach me personally, that Jenny was the person I had complete faith in. Apart from Mickey Bushell and Jade Jones, all the other British wheelchair athletes were in his camp. I understood where he was coming from – after all, wheelchair racing was what he knew. And he was pretty good at the coaching. But when one of your athletes has a world-class coach then, in my view, the job of a performance director is to work with that coach and to support them. Not to bypass them.

Shelly Woods was a good example. Her old coach Pete Wyman guided her to a world record in 2010 but he was soon dumped afterwards for Peter. Put simply, I thought Peter was a bully. There was always the prospect of withdrawing funding and interfering too much and Peter was the UKA's mouthpiece. It pissed me off because he didn't seem to respect what Jenny had done. She was very, very disappointed because he had seen me train only once, so how could he possibly judge the programme we had developed – and, importantly, the programme that had brought me and Great Britain so much success?

For me, Peter's appointment summed up this pointless trend of hiring expensive foreign coaches and I thought it a total waste of money. We have good people here – in Scotland, Liverpool and London. We should develop that coaching talent. I didn't like it when it started happening with the England football team, first with Sven-Göran Eriksson and then with Fabio Capello. For me, it's the same in any sport and as an athlete I was always asking myself where their loyalties really lie. I remember there was a Swiss physio who worked with the British team, and I once noticed them cheering for Marcel Hug in a race. Peter was to deliver for the British Paralympic Team but it didn't feel like that to an outsider at the time.

With one year to go to London, the time had come for decisive action. My shoulder needed urgent treatment and it just wasn't working for me at Lee Valley. I knew that if I was going to fulfil my 2012 ambitions then I would have to go my own way. So, in September, I told UKA I was going back to St Mary's – full time.

The two guys who saved me were my physio, Nick Cooper, and my strength and conditioning coach, Paul Martin. Without them, I doubt I would have achieved what I did in London. I had already chatted to them before I made my decision to leave Lee Valley. I told them I had one year to go and that I was in a mess. Until I got my shoulder fixed I knew I wouldn't be able to train properly. I was desperate for their help.

The problem was that no one was going to pay them. Although St Mary's is part of the English Institute of Sport, UKA told them they weren't prepared to support me financially if I decided to seek alternative back-up away from Lee Valley. It was ridiculous. They were telling me they couldn't afford £30 or £40 for an hour with the best physio I had ever worked with. I asked Peter about it and he said he had no problem with me working out of St Mary's. But then when it came to finding the money, it just didn't happen.

In the end I said I would just fund it out of my own pocket. By this stage it was just too important. At the same time, Paul said the college and the English Institute of Sport were prepared to let him treat me in his lunch hour. But what I couldn't understand was why some of the other able-bodied athletes down at St Mary's seemed to be getting their coaching and treatment paid for through official channels. They didn't seem to be sneaking around, twisting people's arms to help them in their lunch breaks. Whenever Mo Farah was back from America, where he now spends most of his time, he was at St Mary's. You can bet there were no questions about the support he was getting down there. Plus I knew for a fact that other injured athletes like Steph Twell were told they could give Lee Valley a miss and carry on working on their rehabilitation at St Mary's. Once again I felt second best.

There were a lot of politics involved and I suspected Peter of being behind most of the problems. So I told him to come down to St Mary's and have a look at the set-up. He'd only been to see me train once and that was almost three years earlier. He'd been to see most of the other athletes, but not me. Eventually, he did come down and have a look. I thought he had been persuaded, that he had been impressed. That was certainly the message which came across before he left. It was only a short while afterwards when I was chatting to one of the physios at Lee Valley that she mentioned that the visit hadn't gone well. I genuinely thought Peter was about to sign off funding for me at St Mary's. Instead it turned out Jenny had received an email from Peter questioning the set-up. He said he was worried about my technique and my position in the chair. That really got up my nose. He had only come to see me once and there he was criticising me. But this was the position I had always used. It had always served me well. I was totally pissed off.

It made me more determined than ever to just get on and do my own thing. When I went back to Paul and Nick at St Mary's, I couldn't even pick up the bench bar because my range was so limited. I thought I was going to have a poor winter because I couldn't lift any weights, but Paul reassured me immediately, telling me not to worry and that in a couple of months I would be lifting weights again. He also told me that he had cringed when he saw I had been given a second cortisone injection. I guess that's why he wanted to help me: he could see I was getting bad advice.

Being back there made me so happy. I felt like a world-class athlete. They loved working with me and would bend over backwards to help me. I told Nick what I'd done and he said my shoulders simply couldn't take what the UKA coaches had been telling me to do. We had to figure out other ways to build my shoulder up without weights. I did a lot of chin-ups and core stuff and had really heavy physio right up until Christmas. Slowly but surely I started to get that range of movement in my arm back. I cancelled all my autumn races, even turning down the chance to defend my title in the New York Marathon. Peter was disappointed, as he had expected me to compete. I just couldn't win. The year before he had blamed New York for my injury; now, when I was still fighting that same injury, he was encouraging me to go to America and compete. I just ignored him. My winter training programme was way more important than another win in New York.

All the rows left me feeling as sore as my shoulder. It became such a battle. I kept asking myself, 'Do UK Athletics not want me to win in London?'

If they did then they had to let me get on with it my way and trust the people I have always trusted. I wasn't asking for thousands of pounds, and after a while I accepted that I felt I would never get treated the same way as the able-bodied guys. For whatever reason, I was being singled out. It just made me even more determined to follow my own course and to work even harder with Jenny to make sure I proved them all wrong in London.

CHAPTER 10

LONDON CALLING

It's five minutes to midnight on New Year's Eve 2011. I am sitting with Emily, Mason and a few of Emily's friends in my living room, watching the TV. Although I am no longer a big drinker, in any other year I might have had a couple of drinks by now. Nothing too heavy, just a few to get in the mood. But not this year. I am stone-cold sober, glued to the telly waiting for the fireworks. As Big Ben strikes twelve, London's skyline explodes colourfully into life. It's all accompanied by the music from *Chariots of Fire*, the tune which would become the soundtrack to Great Britain's Olympic and Paralympic summer.

After ten minutes or so, the fireworks finish, I turn the TV off and put Mason to bed. I then turn in myself. No point in staying up. I have an interview with TalkSport Radio first thing in the morning and, although I'm not training tomorrow, I will be back out there on 2 January. I don't want to take any chances. I want to make the most of every day I have before the Games start. Suddenly, after all the build-up and all the waiting, it's here.

———

Richmond Park is the sort of place most people go to for fun. Not me. It's my office. The place I go to do business most days. I love being there early in the morning when it's deserted and the sun is just coming up.

But that winter it was a harsh place to be. Some days it was minus ten. I would sit there in my car before a training session, thinking, 'What am I doing here?'

Then I thought about all my rivals training and knew that if I didn't perform at the Games then I would end up blaming it on that one session I missed. I couldn't risk it. So I would do whatever I could, even if it was only five or six miles. I have always hated training in the winter – I can't stand the snow and frost. But during that winter there were some days when I simply couldn't get warm, when after a while I lost all sense of touch in my hands. It didn't matter, though, because at least you had done something. It's only when you get on the podium at a Paralympics or a World Championships that you realise how important those days are. And it's only when you get a medal around your neck that you can smile and think back to those horrible winter days in the park. That's what drove me on that winter, just thinking and dreaming about winning in London.

As 2011 turned to 2012 you could feel the excitement building all the time. Everyone seemed to be talking about it. On New Year's Day I went on TalkSport's *Breakfast Show*. I was asked the question that would follow me all the way up to the Games: 'So how many gold medals are you going to win?'

I had worked out my answer to that one very early on, long before Jenny and I sat down in the autumn and worked out that I would go for four – the 800m, 1,500m, 5,000m and the marathon. I had never got four before and knew it would be hard but I thought I would never have a better chance than in front of my home crowd in my home city. That's not what I told TalkSport that morning: 'I will be more than happy if I get one,' I told them.

I wasn't lying to them. If I had ended with just the one, I would have been really pleased and proud. Getting one is massive. But I didn't want to pile even more pressure on myself. If I had said 'I think I can win four' then even more people would have hung those gold medals around my neck. So I played it safe and whenever anyone asked me in the run-up to the Games how many I would win, that was the response they got.

The run-up had been plotted well in advance. Having made the decision to quit Lee Valley in September 2011, I knew what I needed to do and when. I was so much happier back at St Mary's, working with people I really trusted. Those guys really saved me. I spent a lot of time in January working on my strength in the gym and although

I was still quite cautious about my shoulder, it was starting to feel better.

As winter turned to spring, I headed to Portugal for a bit of much-needed sunshine and to test the new £10,000 racing chair which had been designed for me by scientists working for UK Sport and UK Athletics. After the Beijing Paralympics, the head of development at UK Sport came to meet me at St Mary's. She explained that they had a four-year project and some funding to develop the best cutting-edge technology to help me win in London. She said she could help design new suits and helmets but also a brand-new, state-of-the-art chair for 2012. They even had the guys from British Cycling on board to help develop the technology, and engineers from British Aerospace to test the new kit in wind tunnels to make sure it was as efficient and aerodynamic as possible. It all seemed very impressive.

But I have to admit I had my doubts about the whole thing from the start. I have had meetings with Formula 1 and with universities in the past and, frankly, I had heard it all before. I told her, 'Look, if it's going to work then come back in two months and show me something that is going to move forward.'

But she did come back with a plan and it did move forward. It was a great project and I was excited about it. It was all kept very much under wraps.

When I got to see the finished article that April in Portugal, I was really blown away. It was fantastic. The wheels were just something else – the amount of detail was mind-blowing. It was all black and made from carbon fibre. The cage I sit in was made from aluminium. The axle was all flat and it cut through the wind. The push rims on the wheels were also made of carbon fibre and had a petal design which cleverly locked them in tightly so they couldn't move. There were two ceramic bearings put in the wheels to align perfect rolling movement. For the first time the wheels were specifically made for us. Normally we use cycling wheels which are adapted. But these were bespoke, all designed and crafted by the best designers and technicians at British Cycling. At first the project was just for me. But as time went on, other wheelchair racers were offered the chance to have a new chair designed for them. UK Sport wanted to transfer the marginal-gains approach of British Cycling's performance director, Dave Brailsford, to the Paralympics. Brailsford had transformed cycling with his close attention to detail. If there was any little change – kit, bikes, diet, supplements, training, where his team stay, what beds they sleep on, anything at all – then he would introduce it to his athletes.

Work had started on the chair in late 2008 and a lot of money, time and effort went into it. But sadly, in the end, I couldn't use it. It was ready too late. I had told UK Sport that if I was going to adapt to it and get used to it in time for London then I really needed it eighteen months out from the Games. But I was presented with the finished product five months before the Paralympics. I don't really blame anyone: in the end they had to build three more chairs – more than they expected – and other people and organisations got involved and interfered.

The problem for me was that the chair just took too long to get up to top speed. So it was slower than my usual chair. The initial acceleration was not there – maybe it was too stiff. There was no flex in the wheels. I will use it at some point, maybe after the 2013 season, because I don't want to waste it. I felt so bad to reject it given the amount of time and money UK Sport had spent on it. They didn't say anything when I rejected it, they said ultimately it was all about my performance and if I thought it would hinder that then there was no way I should use it. I still used the suit and the helmet they developed for me, so all their hard work didn't go entirely to waste. They accepted it was their fault that they had just got it to me too late. But I wish I could have used it. It looked fantastic on the track.

Technology can obviously have a big influence in Paralympic sport – there are big advantages to be gained if you can get the most out of your kit. And the wheelchair athletes have learned a lot from the cyclists – especially technology-wise. Racing chairs have certainly come a very long way since people started competing in hospital chairs back in the 1940s and '50s.

My chairs are made for me by a company called Draft based in Huntingdon, near Cambridge. They have always been tailor-made and have been adapted and refined over the fifteen years that I have been working with them. By the time I was in my late teens the design had settled on the one which is so recognisable. Two wheels at the back, a seating cage or pod and then a long frame and set of forks holding a smaller front wheel. By the time Draft were making my chairs most frames were made from lightweight aluminium. But the seating then was very different to what we have now. It was essentially made out of webbing and nylon cloths. This meant it was nice and flexible to sit in – very good for beginners trying to get used to the slightly awkward racing position, where you have to lean right forward. But it moved around a bit too much and you got very tired quite quickly.

By the time of the Beijing Games in 2008 most of the elite athletes had switched to a much better seating cage, which consisted of a welded aluminium plate you could rest your knees on, a solid seat with a small cushioned back rest and a pod in which you could secure your feet to stop them moving about. That is pretty much standard issue now, but no two racing chairs are the same. That's because every athlete's impairment dictates the type of adjustments and changes Draft and the other manufacturers have to make.

My physique is pretty square and evenly spread, but others aren't. Depending on their disability and what side of their body is affected, some could be more muscle bound on their left side than their right, or vice versa. Take, for example, an athlete with an impairment on his left side. If he can't use that side, or is less able to use it, then he will have muscle wastage. That means the right side of his body will be much bulkier and that the chair will need extra padding on the left. There are so many different permutations and it takes Draft a lot of fine-tuning to get it right.

The other thing that I have developed is a padded ratchet strap across the small of my back. This pulls my hips forward towards my folded legs when I am in the chair. It stabilises my body and makes me much more aerodynamic. In wheelchair racing you are always looking for the optimum position which allows you to be as streamlined as possible but still in a sufficiently upright position to push down on the rims of your back wheels. It's a complex equation between power and aerodynamics and I did a lot of testing in wind tunnels in the run-up to the 2012 Games. I found there were huge gains to be had by moving lower and further forward but I also discovered that I couldn't go too far forward as I started to lose power. Even now I know I am not pushing as hard as I could do in races, but the advantage from the aerodynamics more than compensates for that.

The chair I race in weighs about 9 kilos with the wheels on. Chairs have actually got heavier over the years because the nylon-and-cloth seating was much lighter. Including the metal cage foot pod has added about 1.5 kilos. But chairs need to be heavier because athletes are getting so much more powerful now, and they have to withstand a lot of stress.

On top of the long frame which runs down to the front wheel is a small set of handlebars. There have been various different styles over the years and they can be adapted for athletes with different levels of hand function but there are essentially two standard shapes. They are obviously essential to steer in marathons and other road races but in track racing the handlebars are only there for an emergency. Instead we use a brilliant gadget known as the compensator. It's housed under the front frame and has two settings – one to go straight, the other for the bend. You might have wondered why you see wheelchair racers leaning forward and smashing the right-hand side of their chair, near the front wheel. Well, we are hitting the compensator and by bashing it, you can guide the direction of the front wheel. As you bash it, a screw locks the wheel into the new position. So hit it on the left-hand side to steer left into the bend and the right-hand side to go back the other way as you come out. Before any race meeting I will go round and do a few laps to work out what degree of turn I need to get round the bends. Once I've worked that out, I set the compensator to the right angle. It's a fantastic device and means that I can go on pushing the rims on the back wheels without having to constantly steer around the bends. If we had to do that we would all be going backwards!

If you look at the markings on an athletics track you will see a line in each lane which indicates when the transition from straight to bend begins. There is another which indicates the start of the transition from bend to straight. As my front wheel hits the line I whack the compensator and the wheel turns. You would imagine that these tracks are pretty standard, but they aren't. They can really vary so you have to get it right in those warm-ups or you could lose precious time on your rivals.

The only other gadget I have on my chair is a cordless speedometer which gives me my current speed and average speed for any event. It also gives me the time I started, which is mostly useful for marathons. A lot of the guys use GPS systems, which can track where you are and compare where you were at certain times, but I don't bother with that. I am more old school in that sense.

All in, my chair is worth just under £5,000 with the wheels. And the wheels are a third of that cost. That's because they are made from expensive carbon fibre and are specifically designed for wheelchairs. In fact, there are only three companies in the world that make the back wheels and one in the world that makes them for the front.

In time, I am pretty sure a lot of the British guys and developed nations will be using carbon fibre frames. That will make them a little lighter but the main advantage will be that they will be much stiffer. When you're racing you punch the wheels with incredible, repetitive force. This causes the wheels, which are set at an angle of 12 degrees, to deflect. This in turn causes them to rub on the rubber track, causing high levels of friction. After wind resistance, this is the thing which really holds back wheelchair racers like me. This effect is called scrubbing and during races the wheels scrub sideways as well as up and down. This partly explains why we all love hard tracks. The closer to concrete, the better. But that would never work for the runners, who want the track to be as cushioned as possible. So the only solution available to us for the time being is to develop a less flexible frame, which would reduce the movement as we push the back wheels and therefore impact on the tyres and the wheels. That would in turn reduce that friction, meaning we could go even faster.

After fifteen years of working with me I obviously wanted Draft – a British company with a proven pedigree – to be involved. But a lot of people – Peter Eriksson included – didn't agree. They wanted to take all the information that UK Sport had pulled together and give it to Top End, an American company. I said, 'You can't ask an American firm to build chairs for British athletes.' I couldn't understand it. It was just another example of me and the establishment not seeing eye to eye.

When it came down to it, the manufacturer made no difference. I couldn't risk the new chair. I decided I would stick with my old aluminium one. It was less stable and less fancy but I wasn't about to take any chances.

As it was, the head of the French Paralympic team claimed I was doping in technology during the Games. I don't know what he was getting at there. The racing chair I had was no different to the ones the French were using. Actually, my wheels were made in France. Sure, I had been training in wind tunnels but anyone can do that. The Swiss have been doing that for years. But then the French said the cyclists' wheels were too round in the Olympics! Maybe the French felt they didn't have the money to compete with us and so couldn't invest in the technology. For me, the French moaning was a tribute to how professional British sport had become. It made me very proud.

I came back from Portugal to get ready for the London Marathon. This race was always a highlight of my season. It's the reason I started competing. But this year it felt like a grand warm-up to the main event. That didn't mean I didn't want to win it, though. I wanted to set the tone for the rest of 2012. Before the race I told my rivals, 'What I'd say to the guys coming to London is that my training is going great and I don't think I've ever felt in such good shape at this point in the year. I'm averaging about 80 miles a week in the chair.'

It was much closer than I would have liked but I just pipped Marcel and Team USA's Krige Schabort to the line for my sixth win. It meant I had equalled Tanni Grey-Thompson's record of victories in London. That meant a lot. Tanni was one of the big reasons I got back into the sport after losing my way at the end of the 1990s. If it hadn't been for her amazing performances in Sydney I might never have come back.

But I also hinted to reporters after the race that 2012 could be my last marathon.

Emily was pregnant again and we were expecting baby number two in October. I told the press, 'There's not a lot of goals left. I'll definitely take a year out after the Paralympics because I want to spend some time with my family.'

I should have learned by now never to try to predict the future.

———

Inevitably, as Games time draws closer the demands on your time from sponsors and the media grow. I accept that it's part of the job, and for most Paralympians the attention is so rare that you have to make the most of it when it comes along. But that doesn't mean that we deserve to be ripped off, either. In May I agreed to do a promotional photo shoot for a company that approached me. They offered me less than £1,000 for a couple of days' work.

Now, that might seem a lot to some people but when you compare it to the sorts of sums the able-bodied guys were getting then it's nothing. I was very disappointed. Ultimately we don't do it for money but when you see what others are getting you start asking questions. I am sure people just imagine we all get the same as the Olympians. It's simply not true.

In the end my agent, Jamie Baulch from Definitive Sports, spoke to them and they agreed to pay me a bit more. You have to fight your corner in those situations. It was a whole day out of my training programme and those were so valuable. I don't want people to think I am not grateful for the support I receive from companies who wish to work with me but it just made me think that, once again, we do get treated a bit like second-class citizens.

Managing all the extra stuff that comes your way in a Paralympic year is always crazy. But this year was like nothing else I had experienced. I was lucky because Jamie was an athlete, and he understands that all commitments have to come second to the training and preparation. So we had a game plan that all interviews and sponsor commitments would be finished by June, allowing me to just concentrate on getting it right on the track.

I tried to limit my racing that summer. I didn't want to overdo it in such a crucial year and with such a big prize waiting at the end. I did a test event in the Olympic Stadium in May. Although the crowd was a bit disappointing – only 2,000 people in an arena which holds 80,000 – it was a good opportunity to try out some new gloves and see how my tyres went on the newly laid Mondo track. Winning didn't matter and, besides, none of the big foreign names were there.

UK Athletics hadn't invited them because they were worrying about giving our rivals an advantage. Earlier in the year the British cycling team had complained about holding a UCI World Cup as a test event in the shiny new London Velodrome. Although it was great for the British team to get a taste of what that venue would be like, it also gave all the other countries a sneak preview. That was a bit short sighted and I think UKA had learned from that.

The racing schedule Jenny drew up was supposed to keep me sharp but not overdo it. But everything nearly came unstuck when I had a bad crash at a meeting in Pratteln in Switzerland. Crashes are part and parcel of wheelchair racing and while they can look shocking they're often not as bad as they look. This one was.

I don't remember too much about it but I know I was at the back of the pack and was putting on a bit of a sprint around a bend when Kurt Fearnley suddenly veered into my racing line. He caught my wheel and I went flying up in the air, hitting my head badly as I crashed back down on the track. Emily was there with Mason and she was really worried. I grazed my temple and was a bit dazed but I was basically OK. I was more worried about my chair. But I admit I was a bit shaken up by it. It did teach me one lesson, though. In London I couldn't take the chance of trying to win from the back of the field.

I learned another valuable lesson when I moved on to another meeting in Switzerland, this time at the Swiss Paralympic Centre in Nottwil. I was racing a 1,500m and I asked Jenny what she thought of the idea of me leading a race from the front to see if I could win from there. I gave it a go.

I felt good out on my own and I was setting a really fast pace but with 250 metres to go Marcel Hug and the whole pack came past me. I must have come seventh or eighth. I knew now that I needed a bit more fitness and endurance. Wise as ever, Jenny told me after the race that she knew that already but it was good I found out for myself.

Peter Eriksson didn't see it that way. He was going crazy. He couldn't understand what I was doing, acting as a pacemaker for such a good field. He felt I should have been winning races myself, not experimenting.

Jenny was really upset by this. She gave him what for.

Afterwards I went up to him and asked him why he had said what he said to Jenny. But he was in denial. He said he didn't have a row with Jenny. I told him, if you want me to win in London you have to leave me to do it the way I want to do it. I never really listened to him. I just listened to Jenny and to myself. We have a good understanding. I am the one in the middle of the race, she can see it from a distance. Others don't get it. When people ask her what my tactics are, she explains that she does talk about it with me but in the end leaves it up to me to work it out. I'm the one in the race, the one in the middle.

These were happy times on the track and at home. Through all those dark winter months having Mason waiting for me at home gave me a real escape from all the pressures of training. And Emily was giving out such good vibes and making me feel really positive. It's become such an important part of my life after all those early years of instability and broken relationships. The fact that she was expecting another baby always brought things back down to earth. Racing and winning in London was important but there were other things in life.

As the clock ticked down we decided to take a little break as a family. So, around my 33rd birthday on 5 June, we all headed to Paris for four days to get away from it all. We went to a spa hotel, did a bit of shopping, went up the Eiffel Tower.

We were having such a nice time – until I got a call to tell me one of my mates had committed suicide. Lewis Pinto was only twenty-four and a promising boxer. I am not sure what went on and I never asked. The family only lived around the corner from me. Whenever I did well he would always be the first one to come and congratulate me. He was a sportsman so he understood how hard you had to work to get to that sort of level. It rocked me for a bit. He was well loved in the community and the funeral was massive. A couple of hundred of us went up the Roundshaw Airfield and lit lanterns in his memory. I am sure he would have come to watch me in London.

———

The Games were now just two months away. London was getting more and more excited. The Olympic Torch relay was working its way around the country and the coverage on the TV and in the newspapers was impossible to ignore. Everywhere you looked there were adverts or posters reminding you that the Games were coming. It was exactly the motivation I needed as I entered my last and most critical phase of training. Having spent so much of my career training in Richmond Park I know the roads like the back of my hand. For London I needed something different to try and take me to a new level and to give me the strength and endurance I needed to win three track events and, at the end of all that, a marathon.

That's when Jenny persuaded a small group of cyclists to help me with my golden mission. Alan Ephgrave is an amputee cyclist, also known as the one-legged wonder. He has been training in Richmond Park for as long as I have, if not longer. He was a top club cyclist in the 1980s before a crash meant he had to have one of his legs amputated. That hasn't stopped him and I can tell you from bitter first-hand experience that he is still pretty quick. Jenny just went up and asked him one day if he would be up for helping me. He agreed immediately. What's more, he said he would ring a few of his old cycling mates to get them to come along too. Before long, there I was, part of an exclusive little peloton whizzing around Richmond Park, training for Paralympic gold.

They might have been in their sixties but their age hadn't slowed them down that much. They could still shift and they helped me get the quality sessions I needed to build myself up for the Games. Alan and the cyclists just pushed me on every day. I thought I used to go fast but when you start training with other people you realise you can go much, much faster. They would sprint and I would have to catch them. Every day it felt like a race. It made me wish I had had them with me all the time.

Of course, there is a limit to how fast you can go. The top cyclists on the tours can hit about 40mph on the flat whereas I can get to just over 23mph in a wheelchair. But what it did was set me targets all the time, pushing me to new limits and giving me not only speed but much more stamina and endurance. Mind you, I think the riders learned a lot from me. They were amazed and shocked at the way I push and can keep going. Even in the park since the Games I have had cyclists come up to me after a session and say it took them half a mile to catch me up because I was travelling so fast.

As the weeks went on I was just getting faster and faster. I was shocking myself. Just before I left to join the team I did a marathon in Richmond Park. My time was 1 hour 28 minutes. That was extremely quick. But I felt so good that I still got up next morning and did another hard session. The cyclists just looked at me and said, 'That's it, Dave. You are ready. You are going to win four gold medals.'

But I didn't want to think like that. I still had to worry about Marcel or Kurt, or the Chinese. Who had they discovered?

That's why I didn't want to go to Portugal with the British team for their pre-Games training camp in August. I didn't want to break my flow, to change my rhythm. Besides, I had already been to Portugal twice that year, first in April to test the new chair and do a bit of training and again in July, to really hit out the hard miles in the blistering heat. Some days it reached 42 degrees and I dropped a lot of weight.

Going off on my own like that had already upset the powers that be at UK Athletics. So I was determined to show them it wasn't a holiday. Although Emily and Mason came with me, I stayed in another hotel away from them.

I just met up with them when I wasn't training – which wasn't always easy as I trained twice a day most days.

Come August, I felt another trip to Portugal would be pointless. I had done all my fine-tuning and my training was going so well. So I sent an email to UK Athletics explaining my decision. I urged them to trust in me and to understand that it was only because I was so determined to deliver for Great Britain that I didn't want to risk anything going wrong so close to the Games. I was facing the biggest ten days of my life and I wanted to do it my way.

My fear of flying also played a big part in my decision to snub the camp. I simply didn't want to get on another plane a week before the Games. The problems I suffered in Beijing because of that extra flight were still fresh in my mind and I just didn't want all the stress.

I know it sounds ridiculous, but it's one of those things that will probably never change. I think it's control. Even when I'm a passenger in a car I get anxious. When I was a kid I didn't have a problem with flying. It's just something that's developed over time.

Every flight is different. Sometimes I will think about it days before, other times it won't hit me until I arrive at the airport. But once I am there I hate every minute of it, the whole build-up. I will do it because I have to but so much stress goes through my body. Sometimes I can be physically frozen to the spot, paralysed by fear. Other times I can't stop moving, jigging around nervously. I have tried hypnotherapy and talking to people about it. I have even thought about going on flying courses. But in the end I don't want to sit next to people who are nervous themselves because that might make me worse.

I can't even blame it on having had a terrible experience on a flight. You hear of planes dropping a hundred feet or of emergency landings. I have never had anything like that. I did have a bad flight from Switzerland to Italy once. The sky was black and it didn't look like it would ever stop raining. We were delayed and delayed and then, suddenly, air traffic control spotted a break in the weather and decided to go for it. This pilot must have made five or six attempts at landing before he gave up and decided to divert back to Zurich, where we had come from. I was with Jenny and although she tried to reassure me once we landed back in Zurich I had made up my mind. I booked a flight straight back to London. I called my dad and told him to collect me from the airport at this time from this flight and then said I would explain when I got home. I was so scared I just wanted to get back. I know this must sound insane and totally irrational because I had to get on another plane to get home, but that was just how I dealt with it.

Whenever I go away I can't ever really relax. I will be sitting in my hotel or I'll be training and all of a sudden, it's back. That feeling of dread. That thunderclap of a heartbeat, a fluttering in your guts.

'Only another two days to go until I have to get back on the plane.'

It can become a huge distraction and I don't want

anything to affect my racing. That's why I now drive to Switzerland for race meetings. I know it takes so much longer and is tiring but once I knew I could do it and got used to driving on the wrong side of the road, it was a no-brainer for me. These days sport is so international, it's a fact of life that you have to travel to compete and to make money. But as an Arsenal fan I do take some reassurance from the fact that Dennis Bergkamp used to get the train or go by road to Champions League matches because of his fear of flying. I am not the only one but there is no question it is something that has held me back in my career and created an extra set of problems to deal with. When I know it's a long haul and it's a bigger plane, I do feel safer. If I am lucky I sometimes get upgraded, and that makes me feel more comfortable.

I wondered whether having kids would make me less nervous. But I am now more worried than ever about getting on a plane with my family. I have not done it yet. I'm too afraid to. When I went to Portugal with Emily and the kids before London, I made sure they went on another plane. I don't think I could get on the plane with all of them in case it went down with all of us on it. I would rather I went and not them. They are so young; they haven't had their lives yet. It's a sad way to think but I also don't want them to see me scared. I might pass my fears onto them. It's mad – people might think of me as this tough guy, the Weirwolf from London. But here I am reduced to jelly by a plane. It's totally irrational. Driving to races in Switzerland is probably more dangerous than flying there. Sometimes I pass these lorries on the motorway and I see them swaying and I know any moment there could be a bad crash. But at least I've got control. And I am not up in the air. I know a lot of my teammates must think my fear of flying is ridiculous. *I* think it's ridiculous. And actually, if it wasn't for that I probably would have gone to Portugal to be part of the team. But my performance had to come first. So I told UKA I would be waiting for them when they got back to Gatwick Airport, fully decked out in my Paralympics GB kit, ready to make that long-awaited journey to the Olympic village.

———

By that point London had of course already been infected with Olympic fever. The Games opened on 27 July and although I was still very focused on my training and being ready for the Paralympics, the Olympics was impossible to ignore. I was totally caught up in it.

From the moment the opening ceremony started I was convinced we were going to pull it off. For years there had been loads of negative publicity, that it was going to be a disaster, that it was going to be rubbish. But after about ten minutes of Danny Boyle's opening ceremony, I felt like crying. I was so happy and proud. I normally don't pay too much attention to these ceremonies. But this one exceeded my expectations. They are normally really cheesy or downright tedious. All right, so a lot of people watching around the world might have found some of it confusing but I loved the way he focused on our rich past, zoning in on parts of our history which involved ordinary people – the marches, the NHS, the industrial revolution. I always loved history but didn't get the chance to study it enough. This ceremony was as much an education as it was a show. I was also really struck by the decision not to use a load of professional dancers. A lot of the people in it were general members of the public and I loved that.

The show was spectacular, especially the giant rings hovering above the stadium. But I couldn't wait for the athletes' parade. I know a lot of people switch off at this point but it's always a special part of the ceremony for me. By this point Emily had fallen asleep in front of the TV. When she stirred about an hour or so later she said, 'Are we near the end yet?' I replied, 'Afraid not ... we are only at E.' It was getting later and later. But I couldn't go to bed and when Chris Hoy came in with the GB flag and I heard all the noise, I just thought, 'Wow, look at this. We've done it.'

We hadn't even raced yet. But I knew we would do well. It was a home Games, we had invested a lot of money, we had a lot of top coaches and I was sure we would win lots of medals and be up near the top of the table.

Once the Games were off and running I was glued to the BBC. I would go off training in Richmond Park in the morning and then come back and watch as much as I could. I am the sort of person who will get into any sport, especially if there's a British competitor in it.

As the drama unfolded I just kept thinking it would soon be my turn. Watching Usain Bolt winning three gold medals again. David Rudisha smashing the world record in the 800m.

And then there was Super Saturday. For Team GB to win three golds that night was incredible. I always thought Jessica Ennis would do it but I couldn't believe the pressure she was under. She was the poster girl of the Games. Her face was everywhere. But I could see she was in perfect shape. To deliver with the whole country expecting you to win is something I can identify with, albeit on a smaller scale. I actually think the heptathletes should get a medal for every one of their seven events they win – it is such a gruelling event. It's like me only getting one gold at the end of the Paralympics for winning four races. I was so happy for Jess; she is just a lovely and down-to-earth person. She has not changed and I don't think she ever will.

All night I was just screaming at the TV. Emily kept telling me to calm down. But how could you with Mo Farah charging down that home straight in the 10,000m? With that race I was watching the crowd more than anything. There wasn't a single person sitting in their seats, and there was just a sea of British flags. And the noise. That sonic boom as he came round that last bend. It was phenomenal, and you could see it lifted him. I couldn't wait to get there myself and I kept thinking, 'I've got that in a couple of weeks.' It drove me on even more in training.

In some ways I don't know why everyone was so

surprised by the crowd. British sports fans travel everywhere to watch sport so it was always likely they would be
even more enthusiastic in this country, at a home Games.
The whole country seemed high on it, everyone smiling
and talking to each other. It was great to be in London at
that time. There were so many fantastic Olympic moments
that it's almost unfair to single any one of them out. Sir
Chris Hoy, the boxers, Andy Murray and then, of course,
Sir Bradley Wiggins. What he achieved in winning the Tour
de France and then coming to London and winning the
time trial was phenomenal. That really took some guts. But
I love his character too: the sideburns, the rock and roll.
It breaks the 'serious' mould you get with most people in
sport. He's exactly what Britain's about.

It was a dizzying sixteen days and I loved being a specta-
tor, watching Team GB do so well and get third place in
the medal table. So many heroes and so many great memories. But I couldn't be too distracted. My time was fast
approaching and I had to be ready.

CHAPTER 11

TEN DAYS, FOUR GOLDS

I was driving across a railway crossing on my way to training in Richmond Park when I saw it for the first time. There, in giant letters, was the Channel 4 slogan which would come to define the spirit of the London 2012 Paralympic Games:

'THANKS FOR THE WARM-UP.'

It really made me laugh. And made me excited, too. Not only because the Games were so close now, but because it was so bold, so confident and so totally unapologetic. For the first time I didn't feel that people were going to come and watch athletes like me out of sympathy. Everyone wanted to be a part of it. There might have been a seventeen-day break between the Olympics and the Paralympics but it didn't really stop. People couldn't wait to get going again. It was just the second half of the same show.

For years I had been dreaming about my home Games.

Ever since Jacques Rogge opened that envelope in Singapore in 2005 and read out London's name my life had been building towards this moment, ten days to define my career in sport.

I wanted to drink it all in, absorb every moment. Even the opening ceremony, which usually I would duck because I was too focused on my first race. This time I was desperate to be there, to march round that track in front of that crowd. Maybe even to carry the Union flag into the Olympic Stadium.

I never got the chance.

The UKA head coach, Peter Eriksson, banned all the track and field athletes from going. I was gutted – a little bit of my heart was ripped out. Peter said it was too close to competition. But I wasn't racing for two days – and we could have been sneaked off or just gone for the athletes' parade. Why couldn't we just do that? Maybe if you had competition the next day, then fair enough.

Yet we had absolutely no say in it, that's what I didn't like. In Beijing we had the option and I was competing the next day and I was feeling rough. On that occasion it made sense for me not to do it. For the home Games, though, we should have had the choice. We could have jumped on a bus or one of the official cars and it would have taken two minutes.

I'm sure I would have had a good shot at carrying the flag as it was voted on by all the members of Paralympics GB. The wheelchair rugby team put my name down even though I wasn't going. In the end, the tennis player Peter Norfolk got the honour and I was delighted for him. He is such a nice bloke, a great athlete, and he really deserved it. And besides I shouldn't moan too much. I got my little bit of glory during the closing ceremony when I brought the GB flag into the stadium.

Although I watched the ceremony on TV with a few of the other lads from the athletics team, I am slightly embarrassed to say I can't remember too much about it now. Stephen Hawking's appearance was inspiring and Seb Coe's speech was very powerful. But once I knew I wasn't going I switched off a bit and just focused on the task at hand. The ceremony was a distraction. I had a mission: something I had never done before in any major championships, never mind a home Paralympics – to deliver four gold medals in just ten days.

Day One: Friday 31 August. 5,000m heats

Usually I am quite relaxed about heats. I might get a few butterflies in big championships but I always expect to qualify. London was also much more straightforward because I only had to go through two rounds, not three. It would have been much harder to consider going for four golds if there had been more qualifying rounds to come through.

Despite that I was still feeling nervous as hell before that first heat, waiting on the concourse under the stadium for our race to be called. Ours was the third race on and I knew some of my big rivals, Marcel, Kurt and Prawat, were in the first two heats and had done well. The one who really worried me was Julien Casoli. He seemed to be flying. As far as my race was concerned, apart from a Chinese racer called Liu Chengming and a South Korean, Hong Suk-Man, it was pretty straightforward – on paper.

Once I was on the track I was fine. The crowd was amazing, it was exactly what I had hoped for. I looked around, trying to spot an empty seat. I couldn't see one anywhere in the stadium. It was just a mass of faces and bodies. The roar almost split my eardrums. It was like a plane taking off. I felt so good, so strong. I was never in any trouble and booked my place in the final on Sunday night with a winning time of 11:28.88. I was on my way.

Day Two: Saturday 1 September. Rest day

I felt very good when I got up on the Saturday morning. It was quite a late heat so I hadn't really eaten properly the night before, just loads of bananas, as I knew I would have to load up on rest days. I didn't read any of the papers. I wanted to wait for that. I called Emily and my mum and dad on the phone and had a bit of a chat. The heat was the only race that Emily came up for. I didn't want her coming all the way over to Stratford in her condition. She was really starting to show by now and with Mason as well it was all very tiring. The thing was, I never even got a chance to see her on the night of the race. I had failed to spot her in the crowd when I came out onto the track and then afterwards I was whisked straight back to the village. It was weird to think she had been in the stadium with all those people and then I was having to talk to her on the phone the next day. She helped keep me calm because already my mind was starting to turn to the final on the Sunday night. My first shot at gold.

Day Three: Sunday 2 September. 5,000m final
From the moment I opened my eyes at 8 a.m. I was nervous. I had major butterflies. This was it. I only had about twelve hours before my first final at London 2012. I was absolutely buzzing, bouncing off the walls in the afternoon. I just didn't want it to go wrong.

I spoke to Jenny. She tried to make me chill out. She told me I was in the best shape she had ever seen. But I was still worrying about Kurt, Marcel, Prawat and the Frenchman Julien Casoli. What sort of shape would they be in? Had I done enough?

It was a very late race. I had a light lunch then I tried to have an early dinner but it didn't happen. I was too anxious to eat. As race time approached I tried not to show what I was feeling inside. It didn't help that everything was running about ten minutes late – it meant I had more time to fret. When we finally got on the track, that was the first time I felt really emotional. I was really struggling to hold it together. By that point it was almost 10.30 p.m. As I did my warm-up laps on the back straight I spotted my mates, Tarick, Ricky and Leon. But I had to look away because I felt they were going to cry. I have never felt that before. I got to the start line and thought, I have to do this for all the people who have come, all those people who have stayed late into the evening to support me.

The race was a bit of a blur. I just tried to stay in a good position in second or third place. I didn't take the front once. When the field started to bunch up I made sure I was in lane two so I could get out.

There were a couple of times when Marcel tried to make a bit of a break and he stretched the field a bit. On lap seven he came around me, trying to send me a message. I just thought, 'What are you doing? I am just going to sit on your wheel and let you take me home.'

This was the fastest man over 5,000m in the world. He totally played into my hands. I sat there for the whole race, just waiting to pounce. I hit the front with about 150 metres to go. I knew I had the sprint finish to beat him. What I didn't know was who was behind me. Who might come and pip me on the line. But there was no one. And as Marcel ran out of steam, I cruised through to win easily in a time of 11:07.65.

As I crossed the line I shouted so much my throat was sore.

It was relief. Sheer relief. Instantly the pressure had disappeared. I had done it – a gold in my home Games. Now I could relax in all the other races and do my job properly. The other racers were worried then. I beat them by a chair's length. That was massive.

Jenny described the race afterwards as perfect. She told

me I had got it right on the biggest night of my life. And she told me that I could now just go and enjoy the rest of the Games.

Unfortunately, my mum and dad weren't in the stadium to see me win that night. UK Athletics messed up all the tickets. I was supposed to get three tickets a day for each of my finals and five for my heats. Because of that, none of my family entered the public ballot. Then, closer to the Games, we were told UKA couldn't get the ticket allocation. They still sorted some tickets out for us but I was angry at not getting the amount we had been promised. It's normal for families of Olympic athletes to miss out on tickets to see their relatives perform. Demand will always be greater than supply. But it was a new problem for Paralympians. Because it was in London everyone wanted to go, so I had already had to disappoint loads of people. To then have to disappoint the people closest to me, the ones who had supported me along the way, really pissed me off.

Still, at least I had my mates in the crowd that night and as I did my lap of honour they came down to the front row to congratulate me. The noise as I went round was amazing. It was just the same as Mo Farah's races. The wave just followed you around. It was like nothing I had ever experienced before. Seb Coe said afterwards that my win in the 5,000m was one of the highlights of the whole of London 2012. I felt so honoured when he said that: coming from a legend of the track like him, it really meant so much.

Because it was the last race of the night, I was stuck in

doping until the early hours of Monday morning. I was so dehydrated that it took me until 2 a.m. to produce a sample. But even though I had to be up again for the 1,500m heats, I didn't care. I knew adrenalin would get me through. By the time I emerged from a deserted stadium, it was too late to get a bus. I had to get a car to take me back to the village. It was about 3 a.m. by the time I walked into the food hall to grab anything I could. I was starving. I hadn't eaten for almost twelve hours. It wasn't exactly textbook diet stuff, a couple of bits of pizza. What a way to celebrate winning gold at your home Games!

When I got back to my room I couldn't sleep. I had so many text messages. I tried to reply to as many as possible and I obviously rang Jenny and Emily. I watched my Twitter feed go crazy. I could sense I had been at the centre of something extraordinary but when you are racing you don't realise the impact. I knew how I felt, though. My adrenalin was flowing, my heart was pumping and I had the biggest smile on my face.

I put on some film or other, I can't remember what it was, and I finally crashed out at about 4 a.m.

Day Four: Monday 3 September. 1,500m heats
I didn't get much sleep that night. With my heat off at 10 a.m. I had to be up at 7 a.m. So it wasn't exactly the best preparation. I had that buzz you get when you haven't had enough sleep. It felt good but I knew I would have to crash out at some point.

In that state there was only one thing for it. I went to the flat above me and had a coffee with Chantal Petitclerc, the UKA team mentor. By the time I got to the warm-up I felt like a new man again.

It was only when I started to see some of the media coverage and talk to people down at the warm-up track that I realised how big my win had been. I also didn't have a clue that the Duchess of Cambridge had been in the crowd cheering me on. When I looked back at the TV coverage I saw how Seb Coe, next to her in the VIP section, had pointed me out and suggested she keep an eye on me during the race. Apparently she hadn't seen a gold medal all day and she has since spoken to me about how I made her night because I delivered the gold medal she had been hunting for. And in the very last race of the night. That really made me very proud.

I also didn't realise until the next morning that, big though my performance was, it had been totally overshadowed by Oscar Pistorius's defeat by the young Brazilian Alan Oliveira in the T43/44 200m. It was the upset of the Games so far: Pistorius, the biggest name of the Games, beaten by this kid in the last 20 metres of the race. That morning people kept coming up to me saying, 'So I see Oscar's stolen your limelight again.'

I honestly didn't know too much about it. I had been so focused, thinking about my final, that I had missed the row that was brewing a few yards away from me. After Oscar lost he came into the mixed zone, where journalists can grab the athletes for interview, and told the TV cameras that the International Paralympic Committee should check the length of Oliveira's prosthetic legs. He told reporters, 'I'm not taking away from Alan's performance, he's a great athlete, but these guys are a lot taller and you can't compete with the stride length. You saw how far he came back. We aren't racing a fair race.'

Once again the Paralympics was becoming the stage for the Oscar Pistorius story. During the Olympics, whenever British athletes won they got on the front and back pages. I thought I was going to get the same treatment that morning. But Oscar blew all that.

I don't know Oscar well at all. Our paths have crossed occasionally and we would always say hello to each other, but not much more beyond that. I've always thought he seems a nice bloke and obviously an amazingly gifted athlete.

What's gone on since the Games is as astonishing to me as it is the rest of the world. But I just don't know him well enough to judge. When the story broke that he had shot his girlfriend the media kept calling me up and asking me to comment. But what could I say? I didn't have a clue what had gone on and didn't know him.

But when it comes to his quest – successfully fulfilled to such acclaim in London – to become the first male Paralympian to run in the Olympics, well, I do have an opinion. On one level I can understand where he's coming from – he wants to compete and be the best he can be. He thinks he can run against able-bodied athletes. If I was in his situation I would probably want to do the same thing.

And yet when he runs in the Paralympics, gets beaten and then moans about it, well, then I see a different side. At first I was fully backing him. Why not? He didn't have a massive advantage – all right, he can't get calf strains and maybe doesn't get lactic acid build-up, but he's never going to win a gold medal in the Olympics. He's not even going to make an individual final because he's not quick enough. Forty-five seconds was his best but you have to be in the high 44s to make a final. But if that was what he wanted to do I backed him.

Then when you see him lose to Alan Oliveira in the Paralympics and start moaning, you stop and think, hang on. Oscar had been moaning for years about a lack of competition in the Paralympics. It was one of the reasons he was so determined to run in the Olympic Games. Now someone like Oliveira or our own Jonnie Peacock comes along and you have got the competition you wanted and you suddenly complain about that. What does he want? To wipe the floor with everyone in the Paralympics and then do OK in the Olympics? You just can't have the best of both worlds. You start wondering whether it is all just a publicity stunt.

As the row rumbled on I was pretty confident – for once – that the IPC had called this one right. All the runners with blades get measured beforehand and I am confident they strictly enforced the rules. I know from being in the call room before races in London that it was extremely strict. Alan Oliveira wouldn't have been allowed on the track if there were any question marks about the length of his blades, if they thought he was cheating or his legs were too long. My British teammate Richard Whitehead experienced the same thing during the World Championships in Christchurch. There was a big hoo-ha then because he came out of the woodwork and beat everyone. Loads of people started pointing the finger at him, saying, how has he done that? Are his blades too long?

This debate will only get really difficult if a blade runner emerges who can run fast enough to win gold in the Olympics. But I don't think for one minute that the International Olympic Committee or all the other able-bodied athletes would allow it. Do you think if Oscar was a real threat to the able-bodied guys that they would let him in? At the moment it's all very matey, but let's see how friendly everyone is if a Paralympian starts running sub-45 seconds.

It's very difficult to know where to draw the line. Obviously Oscar is a fantastic athlete and to run in the Olympics is an amazing achievement, but look at wheelchair racers like me. We would never get the chance Oscar got. The best I could have hoped for would have been an exhibition race during the Olympic Games. I really pushed on that but the IPC didn't want to do it. It was always a tradition going back years and I thought the 1,500m, as one of the blue riband events of the Paralympics, should be the one to get in. But it never got off the ground. The IPC – rightly, I guess – wanted our Games to be the main event. By staging an exhibition in the Olympics it was effectively admitting that we were second best, not parallel.

But what if you looked at things the other way around? What if an able-bodied athlete jumped into a wheelchair and started competing against us? Technically, our class, T54, is open so is there anything to stop that? It's a real grey area.

Actually, I wouldn't be too worried if someone able bodied did take us on because it is ultimately about technique and power in my class. It might sound strange but walking is a disadvantage because you build up leg muscle weight and that bulk means you are much heavier. And if you are heavier you are slower in your chair. Besides, the real power all comes from the arms and the shoulders. It's an interesting debate but I suspect it will remain that – a talking point.

As for Oscar and his latest drama, I had to just put all that to one side and qualify for the final of the 1,500m. I had a really tough heat with Prawat and Marcel up against me. There was also the lightning-fast Chinese athlete who had beaten me in the 400m in Beijing, Zhang Lixin. Only the first three were guaranteed a place in Wednesday's final, plus perhaps a fastest qualifier. The pressure was on.

I sat behind Marcel for much of the race but then Prawat was on my back wheel waiting to take me on. The only way I could qualify was if I pushed Marcel all the way. I knew Lixin was closing on me too, so it was really tight. In the end I scraped through in third in a time of 3:11.35. Afterwards there was a real heart-in-mouth moment when we had to wait for the scoreboard to flash up the official results. I knew I had come third but I started to think there was a problem. Maybe one of the judges had spotted something. The whole crowd were silent waiting for my name to pop up in third with that big 'Q' indicating I had qualified next to it. I had to move on to the mixed zone and I was actually on TV being interviewed when the big roar went up confirming I was in. I tried to pretend that it was all part of some grand plan, but it wasn't. Physically I was actually fine but mentally I was a bit tired.

With my place in the 1,500m final secure, I could finally look forward to getting my hands on my first gold medal. The presentation ceremony for the 5,000m was scheduled for the end of that morning session. And I was so touched that 80,000 people waited behind to see it and to sing 'God Save the Queen' with me. In between my heat and the presentation I managed to nip off and have a quick shower and change into my tracksuit. I was hoping it might make me feel a bit fresher. But as I was waiting to be taken into the stadium with Julien Casoli, I was feeling really nervous, hot and exhausted.

Once I got onto the podium and had that medal around my neck the roar was unbelievable. I had never really held a London medal before now. I had seen them but I was a bit suspicious about getting too close as I didn't want to jinx myself. So to hold one of those bad boys was brilliant. It felt weighty. Some of the medals you get at championships feel like they've been bought from Poundland. This didn't: it was massive and felt like a just reward for all the months, all the years, of hard work.

I know this will sound daft, but I made sure I learned all the words to the national anthem off by heart before the Games. I know it's very short and there aren't a lot of words to learn but I just didn't want to slip up. And I wanted to show people how patriotic I was and how much it mattered to me. The whole stadium seemed to be singing with me as the Union flag rose. Of course you dream of this moment but now I was there it didn't feel strange or surreal. It just felt right. Like I belonged there.

For months now I had been telling people that I would be happy to get just one gold in London. But that wasn't how I felt now. I wanted more.

Day Five: Tuesday 4 September. 1,500m final
That morning I surprised myself. Normally, the day of a final would be really nervy and anxious. I expected to feel the same way as I had on the Sunday. But I just woke up feeling a great sense of calm. It was as if a huge weight had been lifted from my shoulders. I must have been giving out really confident vibes, because when I got down to the warm-up track that evening I could see a couple of the other guys looked a bit scared of me. As we did a few laps some of them tried to match me for pace but they couldn't. I left

them for dead. I looked at their faces and I could see how worried they were.

Down at the warm-up track word reached me via the former Canadian racer Jeff Adams, who was in London commentating, that Kurt Fearnley had been highlighting some flaws in my performance in the 5,000m. I was a bit puzzled to hear this. If I had some flaws then how did I win so convincingly? It was probably just Kurt playing mind games and I didn't really mind. People try to beat you in all sorts of different ways.

I was still feeling relaxed as we lined up for the start. When the gun went it was the Chinese athlete Liu Yang who made the early running. He was a bit of an unknown quantity. But I wasn't too concerned. If it had been his teammate Lixin then I might have been a bit worried. As expected, by the end of the lap he fell away.

I positioned myself in my usual place, in lane two in second or third place, poised to strike, staying out of trouble. Then, as we approached lap three, Josh Cassidy of Canada came up to me on the outside. At first I was a bit cautious because I didn't know who it was. I worried about getting boxed in. But he shouted across to me that he wasn't going to do that. Because Josh and I are friends I was pleased he was there next to me. He was the best person to be there at this point. Although we are rivals we were helping each other out.

As for my big rivals, Kurt and Marcel, I had no idea where they were. I only found out when I watched it back that Kurt was stuck at the back, having the worst race I have ever seen him in.

As Thailand's Saichon Konjen chased Yang down I stayed on his wheel. Then, on the last lap, I found myself in the perfect position with his teammate Prawat on the outside of me. I decided to go for it with a lap to go. I didn't want to wait. I opened up as much as I could on the back straight and took the lead with about 300 metres to go. If you look back at the TV pictures my arm speed appeared the same as the others but I was just pulling away from them all the time. I was in another place – the noise from the crowd just lifting me, pushing me on and on to the finish. Usually you feel a little bit tired going into the home straight, but I didn't. I kept hammering it until I crossed the line, winning gold in a time of 3:12.09. Prawat was second and the Korean Kim Gyu-Dae got bronze.

Just like Sunday night and the 5,000m, the Olympic Stadium erupted in joy. I went crazy, waving my arms around and punching the air. It was such a powerful feeling to be the conductor of this amazing noise. And now to have two gold medals! I looked around at all these faces, boys and girls screaming their heads off, going nuts. I saw my friends again, Leon, Tarick and Ricky. I remember them leaning over the front rail but I couldn't get close to them. Ricky said later he could see I was in the zone and just welling up.

As I worked my way through the mixed zone it seemed the press pack asking me questions had grown a lot since

Sunday night. You had your regulars like Gareth A. Davies of the *Telegraph*. He has always been around for my big races and is such a great supporter of Paralympic sport. I can remember him putting up four fingers after that race, telling me I would go on and win all four gold medals. But there were also lots of new journalists there, showing interest for the first time. I felt really flattered that some of these big writers and journalists were now, in this incredible summer of British sport, focusing their attention on me.

With the medal ceremony happening the same night as the final I didn't have much time to do anything. I hadn't eaten for hours so I tried to get a quick bite, whatever I could grab, energy bars, Lucozade, anything. It didn't matter, though. I couldn't wait for this ceremony. I didn't have any nerves this time. I just enjoyed every moment and belted out 'God Save the Queen' at the top of my voice. Again, I wanted to show people how much I cared about competing for my country.

I tried to unwind afterwards. As an athlete in the middle of a schedule like mine, you couldn't afford to switch off too much. The heats of the 800m were the next day and I had to move on quickly. I couldn't wallow in the emotion of it all. It was just eat, sleep, drink and get yourself ready for the next race. I knew Thursday was a big night for Paralympics GB and I wanted to make sure I got the heat right.

I went over to the warm-up track to see Jenny. She never

goes into the stadium to watch me in big races. She is superstitious in that way. She thinks she might put a jinx on me or something. She has taken some stick for it over the years. It was only when Lloyd Cowan, Christine Ohuruogu's coach, came up to her and said, 'Don't worry, I do the same thing,' that she felt a bit more at ease about it. She can see everything better on TV and she doesn't get caught up in the emotions.

When we met up she gave me a massive hug. She kept saying we had proved everyone wrong. She felt she could walk around with her head held high and whatever anyone else said it didn't matter. I just wished Emily was there too, but I didn't want her to come up to the stadium. My finals were always late and with Mason it just meant a lot of hassle.

When I eventually got back to my room I remember taking a picture of my two gold medals and sticking it on Twitter. I just left it at that – I didn't write anything to go with the picture. I didn't need to. I then closed them away in the drawer by my bed, locked it and went to sleep. Even at that point, with two already banked, I wasn't thinking, 'I can get four.' I was just thinking of the next race.

Day Six: Wednesday 5 September. 800m heats
I was now halfway through. I had two golds and I had broken the back of my schedule. I just had three more days of racing. I didn't feel too bad, pretty strong. That day I knew I had a tough heat. Kurt and Marcel were with me

in the second of three heats and only the top two could go through to the final, plus a couple of fast losers. This time I didn't take any chances. I hit the front earlier than usual and looked back to see where Marcel and Kurt were and they were a long way back. Kurt didn't make it. He came third and missed out. I never expected that. He was the 800m silver medallist in Beijing and I just always expect him to be alongside me in the big finals. As for me, I was just cruising and won easily in a time of 1:37.09 – a good second and a bit ahead of Marcel. At that point I did start to think I could get three gold medals and better my two from China in 2008.

Because the heat was all done and dusted by 10.30 a.m. I had the rest of the day to chill out and try and get some rest, take on some food and try to prepare for what would be the most memorable night of the London Paralympics.

Day Seven: Thursday 6 September. 800m final

If the Olympic Games had 'Super Saturday', then the Paralympics had 'Thriller Thursday'. Even before the athletics started that night Paralympics GB had won three gold medals – Josef Craig in the pool, Sarah Storey in the velodrome and Helena Lucas in a keelboat. The athletes had the chance to double that tally with Hannah Cockcroft in the T34 200m, Jonnie Peacock in the T44 100m and yours truly in the T54 800m.

It was also the night when the Weirwolf legend really took off. The whole thing started with the C4 presenter Rick

Edwards. He came up with the nickname on the Paralympic show a few years earlier. We were doing a competition with able-bodied guys who worked in the sports business. One was a body builder, one a lifeguard and one a gymnast. The challenge was for them to get in a racing chair and beat me over 100m. As a bit of a laugh, Rick gave everyone WWF wrestling-style nicknames. I think the bodyguard was called 'The Unit' and that was when he suggested calling me 'Weirwolf'.

Then, during the Games, Rob, one of the team doctors, found an old song by a rock singer, Warren Zevon, called 'Werewolves of London'. It wasn't to my usual taste but it has a couple of funny lines like 'There was a hairy-handed gent who ran amok in Kent' and a catchy chorus you can howl along to. I have to admit I quite liked it and once Rob posted it online it took on a life of its own.

Before I knew it, it was all over the place and some-one in the team had tracked down some werewolf masks from somewhere (God knows where in the middle of a Paralympic Games) and brought them down to the stadium for the final of the 800m. They even played the song in the stadium that night. I came to really like it. After all, Usain Bolt had the lightning bolt, Mo had the Mo-bot, Wiggo had his sideburns and mop top and now I was the Weirwolf. I have always loved the way British sport creates big characters.

I had to try not to get carried away with all the excite-ment and attention. The 800m was possibly the toughest of all my track races in London and I planned to go for it from the start. To treat it as if it was a 400m race.

After the first bend I was level with Zhang Lixin, which was really good. I knew he would be the fastest so I just sat on his back wheel. Behind me there was a bad crash involving America's Jordan Bird, my mate Josh Cassidy of Canada and the Frenchman Julien Casoli. It was quite a bad one and Julien didn't finish in the end. Fortunately, I was out of trouble because Lixin was pushing quite hard.

It was only then that I noticed my zip had come down on my top and I was exposing my chest to the world. I have no idea what happened to it but all of a sudden the top was flapping around. I was thinking, 'This isn't very aerodynamic.' All those days in wind tunnels testing helmets and your chair, only for your zip to break and slow you down. There was nothing I could do. I couldn't stop to do it up. I had to push through it.

I was feeling quite tired and drained but as we hit the final lap the roar went up. Lixin was pushing 22mph on the final bend and I was just praying he wasn't going to go faster. I opened up off the back of the last bend and my speed stayed the same all the way down the home straight. Lixin started going backwards. He just faded as he hit the home straight but I felt I was never going to fade.

Then I was worried about Marcel. Normally you will see a wheel creeping up on your outside. But it didn't happen. No one got near me.

People might think that after you win one or two golds,

the impact of another one doesn't feel quite so special. I can assure you the opposite is true. It just feels better and better. If you look back at the replays of the finish and my victory lap, I cross the line and then start waving my arms around like a maniac, really enjoying the moment. Then all of a sudden I start fiddling with my top again, trying to fix it and pull the zip up. I know it might sound silly but I just felt a bit self-conscious. It took me ages to get a grip and do it up.

That was when I saw my mum and dad in the crowd, but I couldn't get over to them. They were crying and everyone was turning to them. The nice thing about that is that they actually had tickets for much higher up and some other friends swapped with them so they could be closer to the track in case I won and they could get to see me afterwards. I know my mum and dad were so grateful for that, it was such a nice gesture. My mum asked me afterwards if I couldn't see them. She said my eyes were just black, as if I was in another world. It was a surreal moment. I kept wondering if I was ever going to wake up. I eventually got over to them, but I only had seconds because the officials were rushing us on. They were hassling me to get over to the mixed zone to do my interviews. That was actually the first time I spotted the group of team members wearing the werewolf masks. At one point my Welsh teammate Aled Davies took his mask off. When he did I could see he was in tears. It was a very touching moment – to see your own teammates so moved by what you had achieved.

It was such an extraordinary night to be involved in. Before I raced, Hannah had already won gold in the 200m, and I was still talking to the cameras in the mixed zone at the side of the track when Jonnie Peacock won in the 100m – against Oscar Pistorius. There had been so much hype and attention over the previous couple of days. He was only nineteen, and he must have felt under enormous pressure.

And then there was a false start. If that had been me at his age I would have been a bag of nerves. But he raised a finger to his lips and *SSSSHHHHHDDDD* the crowd. I was very impressed. He could have gone to pieces. The crowd was shouting his name over and over again. I knew at that point we had really captured the imagination of this public.

Jonnie's race was the only race I watched live in the whole Games. I just so wanted to watch a British athlete wipe the floor with Oscar. He was the world record holder, under pressure. To see Jonnie cross that line and see him overwhelmed and elated was just brilliant.

We both got our medals that night and while we were waiting we gave each other a big hug.

I got my medal from the comedian Eddie Izzard. He just said, 'Bloody brilliant.' And then singing the national anthem for a third time in that stadium – everyone joining in, belting it out with such pride. I never got bored of it.

I didn't even get drug tested so I didn't spend the next three hours sitting in a room waiting to pee. A lot of people might find it surprising that the winner of a Paralympic gold medal didn't get automatically drug tested. But the anti-doping officials said there was no point – I had already been tested three times since the Games started, once in the village when I arrived and then after the 5,000m and the 1,500m.

So far I haven't come across performance-enhancing drugs in wheelchair racing. That doesn't mean I haven't come across suspicion. Back in 2006 and 2007, when I was breaking world records, I knew people would be asking themselves how I was doing it. But it was just pure training. And besides, I am probably the most tested athlete in Paralympic sport. During the 2006 World Championships I was tested two or three times a day.

I actually welcome that. The more you are tested the better, as far as I am concerned, because it shows you aren't on drugs. That's not to say the system is perfect. Far from it. You can figure it out. If I went on a training camp they would test me before I went or when I came back. Sometimes both. A week before the marathon I would always get tested and then in the marathon itself. Leading into a big championships I would get tested two or three times.

I don't think that's enough and it's too predictable. But the thing that really annoys me is the lack of consistency. Every single country that competes in the Olympics and Paralympics should do the same level of testing as us. Then it would be fair. America, Canada, Australia – they do it. But lots don't have the systems in place. And I know what WADA (the World Anti-Doping Agency) and the other anti-doping agencies will say: lots of smaller countries don't have the money. Well, WADA should take it on, then. They must have the money.

Having said that, I do think most Paralympians are clean. And in wheelchair racing we are, on the whole, honest people who love racing each other. There are always other ways to improve that 1 or 2 per cent: technology and good diet – like the cycling team has done for years and years. There are alternative ways to putting dope in your system.

When you are seeing all these athletes getting caught in the Olympics, it makes me angry. And I do think the Olympics are dirtier than the Paralympics. Maybe there's more at stake, greater competition.

I know some people are suspicious of the Paralympians because a lot of the athletes have to take medication. But what can they do? As long as they aren't using them to cheat.

For once I was back to my room nice and early. But, irritatingly, I couldn't sleep. I was still up at 4 a.m. I might as well have done a drugs test. I just couldn't drop off. So I got my London 2012 duvet from my bed, went into the living room and sat on the sofa watching the BBC news channel. For the first time in a week, I didn't have anything to do the next day – or the day after. That was perhaps why I was still wide awake, buzzing from probably the most incredible night British Paralympic sport has ever seen.

Day Eight: Friday 7 September. Rest day

I was so exhausted when I woke up on Friday morning. Part of me felt that my job was done. But I so wanted that marathon. I now had two complete days of rest to try and rebuild my strength for that race.

Later that day I was meeting Emily and Mason in the family zone at Team GB House, Westfield. It was the first time I had done that during the whole Games. She got lost, bless her, and she was quite upset about it all, especially being pregnant. She got off at the wrong tube stop.

Once she met me she was OK. She had been so anxious to see me – it was more than two weeks since we had been together. She said she was worried I might have to rush off for some reason. But I reassured her that I would be spending the whole day with her. It was so good to see my little boy. He had started walking on his first birthday, about six weeks earlier, so he was tottering around GB House. Emily had asked me to bring my medals with me to show them off. I opened the bag and took them out and put them on the table. She picked them up and put them on. And then she said, 'Now for number four, Dave.'

I didn't say anything but in my mind I was thinking, 'I am so tired.' I just said I would give it my best shot.

Then she proceeded to tell me about how I was everywhere and how everyone on the estate was talking about me. I couldn't believe the number of people who were planning to come up to town for the marathon.

By this point she was really showing with Tilly. She only had a month to go. But throughout the Games I was worried the baby might come early. Mason had. I was always ringing home to make sure Emily was OK. I felt like I should have been there and helping but this was a once-in-a-lifetime thing.

When it came time to say goodbye to her and Mason it was really tough, but I only had two more days to go so that kept me going. Having had such a horrible journey across London I made sure she didn't get a train back this time. The security guard who was looking after me took her down to where she could get a black cab to take her all the way back. I gave her £60 or £70 to get home.

I then headed back to the village, got a bit of dinner and crashed out.

Day Nine: Saturday 8 September. Rest day
I still felt really tired and drained. By this point it was too late to pull out of the marathon. At lunchtime all those doing the marathons had to pack up and move to a hotel around the corner from St James's Park. It was strange to be out of the village. I spent most of the afternoon checking my chair – making sure my tyres were road ones and that everything was set up just right for the 26.2-mile course. The weather was really hot and I was anticipating having to compete in temperatures above 27 degrees. Suddenly I was glad I had done all that work in the sweltering heat of Portugal in July. It was going to come in handy.

But because it was going to be so hot, it left me with a bit of a dilemma about what to wear. I'd had a short-sleeved suit made for me but up until this point I had worn my long-sleeved one and it didn't feel right to change anything that had been working.

Day Ten: Sunday 9 September. The marathon
I felt good when I woke up, much better than the previous two days. This was new territory for me, though, and it was quite strange to deal with from a psychological point of view. Normally at this stage my work was done but now I had to get myself going for one more race day. And not any old race: the biggest of them all.

Because we were staying just around the corner from the start and finish line I decided to put all my kit and spare parts on a bus and push myself down to the start in my chair. Just before going to line up I popped into the official organisers' tent. It was there I bumped into my hero Heinz Frei. He was competing in the marathon too, but this was the first time I had seen him because he had been doing hand cycling at Brands Hatch for the rest of the Games. It was such a good moment to see the man who had convinced me to take up the sport as a kid. He congratulated me on what I had achieved and told me he thought I was amazing. To hear that from him was such an honour. It gave me such an enormous lift.

I had studied the marathon course quite a bit over the previous few days. I got a DVD and zoned in on the sections of the course that looked tricky. They were all stored in the memory bank.

The race started with a small loop of about 2 miles. It didn't go off that quick and by the time it came back around to the point by Buckingham Palace where all my friends and family were, I had enough time to hear them yelling me on. I could also see all the werewolf masks in the crowd. It was an incredible feeling to know that all these people were screaming and shouting for me.

But after about 3 miles it started to go wrong. I just lost the plot. I felt like I was dying. For a while I seriously considered just pulling over to the side and giving up. But something inside me told me not to. I had to grit my teeth and get through this bad patch. I couldn't let the crowd down and I didn't want to let myself down. This was the race I wanted to win the most. But the loss of energy seemed to go on for a lifetime.

I had a shot of beetroot juice just by my knees and although the plan was to have it at 16 miles to give me a late lift, I had to take it there and then. That was my last chance to get some energy in my body so I took it. I prayed it would work.

About 6 or 7 miles in, I felt like I was getting back to normal. But for a while it was really touch and go. I figured that as long as I kept it together, raced my normal race, then I would be in with a shout.

Up front Kurt was trying to make a break for it. But, unusually, I didn't panic. Normally I chase them down because I worry they might get too far ahead. This time I stayed calm. I just had this feeling I would be able to chase Kurt or anyone else down.

The race was still young but already I was going through a rollercoaster of emotions. At one point I was in a mess and almost pulling out, the next I was just relaxing and letting people get away from me.

As the race entered its final stages I noticed Marcel and Kurt were talking a lot. I wondered whether they were trying to come up with a plan to beat me by teaming up. I couldn't be sure that was what was going on but it made me even more determined to win. It put some real fire in my belly.

As we raced past Tower Bridge for the last time, it was time to make my move. At this point – about 23 miles in – the course switches back on itself and heads back west, away from Docklands. The course also climbs slightly. This was the moment to push the field as hard as I could. I wanted to see if I could get about half a mile ahead. This late in the race I figured a real burst of speed could hurt the likes of Marcel and Kurt.

Then, after a while, I sat up and let them catch me, but I knew it had worked.

Kurt and Marcel were tiring and I was feeling stronger and stronger. The only question that remained now was whether I had the energy reserves to produce a big sprint finish.

As I approached that final bend by the palace I could

hear my friends and family screaming me on. I had always planned to be in front going into that bend, and I knew I had a higher top-end speed than the others. I also felt comfortable because it was very similar to the sprints I had been doing in Richmond Park. So I just imagined I was back there.

I hit that bend and went for it. Kurt and Marcel gave chase but I was too fast; I opened a lead of 300 metres as I approached the finishing line. And the remarkable thing is that my speed was going up and up. I was hitting 24mph. I couldn't believe the speed I was doing. I just gritted my teeth. I couldn't afford to ease up.

When I cross the line I usually celebrate and hold my arms in the air, but I didn't do that during the Paralympics. Why? Well, there was no tape to break through, so I couldn't be sure where the finishing line was. There was quite a long period where I didn't know where the line was. I was disorientated, so I pushed for a good 10–20 metres extra, playing it safe. I was actually worried I hadn't finished and that I might have to do another lap. It was only when the lead car pulled over that I knew we had finished.

I asked the organisers afterwards, where was the tape? They told me they couldn't have any for the wheelchair races because of health and safety regulations. Have you ever heard anything more ridiculous? I have broken the tape in races hundreds of times and I am still here to tell the tale.

Afterwards Marcel and Kurt were great sportsmen and came up to me and told me I had been the greatest. Simply unbeatable. That was nice because you do everything to beat people and win. But I believe you can behave like gentlemen afterwards. I told Marcel, 'Don't worry – your time will come.' If he gets it right in the next Games he will be unbeatable.

After they left me, I was sat there just talking to myself like a madman. I didn't know whether to warm down or what. I was in another world. That's when I started to cry a little bit. All week I had wanted to cry but I had just about held it together. Then I went back to the organisers' tent afterwards and I saw the disability coordinator of the London Marathon, Michelle Weltman. She put her arms around me and I collapsed in tears. I kept muttering, 'I can't believe it. I've done it.'

I didn't even get out of my chair. I couldn't. I was just sat there crying. Exhausted. Elated.

Then Tanni came in and put her arms around me. She looked shell shocked. I told her about how the beetroot juice had kept me going during the early stages when I thought I might have to pull over and quit. Unfortunately, Boris Johnson, who was there to present the medals, heard all this and wandered over. He asked me to repeat what I had told Tanni about the beetroot juice. He couldn't believe his ears. He kept saying, 'Are you serious? Beetroot juice did that for you?'

I explained that for energy it was much better than

coffee, and healthier. But I told him on the basis that he would keep it a secret. Fat chance. He used it as one of his little jokes in his speech during the Heroes Parade around London the next day. All I can say to the Mayor of London is: 'Thanks a lot, Boris!'

I eventually pulled myself together, got changed and got my phone out to try and track down Emily and the rest of my family. But first I had to get my fourth and final gold. The most precious of the lot.

I couldn't wait to get on that podium by Buckingham Palace. It was such a great backdrop. Then, after the ceremony finished, all the photographers were asking me to pose for pictures and I had to ask them to wait a minute while I went to see my family. I still hadn't seen them.

When I found them all – Emily, Mason, my mum and dad and friends – I gave everyone a massive hug and then Mason jumped on my lap. The photographers weren't going to miss that. So they asked me to wheel out to the middle of the road with him on my knees to have our photo taken. I was a bit worried he might cry because he seemed to be under the weather and in fact after that he was ill for a few days. But he sat very still and calm for that photograph. The result is a picture that I will always treasure: Mason sat there in his Great Britain shorts, me holding a Union flag above our heads, the shiny gold medal around both our necks. I have had it put on a giant canvas in my front room and I have another, close-up, version on my stairs.

After hanging around in doping for ages the officials let

me take my gold medal back to the village and have my test there. It had been such a hot day and I was so dehydrated that I just couldn't produce. And I was running out of time.

That evening I had to go straight over to GB House in Westfield to get ready for the closing ceremony. It had just been announced that Sarah Storey and I would be carrying the flag into the stadium. That was such an honour and, although it had only been a couple of days, I couldn't wait to get back into that stadium one last time.

When I walked into the room it was packed with about 300 people from Paralympics GB and everyone gave me a massive cheer. That's when I had my first beer in about fifteen months. As you might imagine, it tasted very, very sweet. Then I had to go back to where we were staying in the village for a team meeting. I was still in my racing gear, while the rest of the team were kitted out for the closing ceremony. After a few minutes I had to put my hand up and ask if I could go and have a shower and be on my own for five minutes.

Once I was alone I tried to take in everything that had just happened to me.

The only way I can describe it is that it felt like a story I was playing a part in. Even now I feel like someone is going to wake me up and tell me it's time to race.

But it did happen. I did win those four gold medals. I did carry the Union flag into the stadium for the closing ceremony. And what made it really magical for me was the fact that I had won the very last gold medal of the London

Olympic and Paralympic party. That was something I had really wanted to do from the word go. In the future, when the question is asked, 'Who did that?', I will be able to say it was me. I had become part of British sporting history.

CHAPTER 12

SO, WHAT DIFFERENCE DID IT MAKE?

'In this country we will never think of sport the same way and we will never think of disability the same way. The Paralympians have lifted the cloud of limitation.'
– Sebastian Coe, Paralympic closing ceremony speech, Sunday 9 September 2012

For so many years people were frightened to ask me why I was in a wheelchair. They always assumed I had been in an accident. Those who did pluck up the courage were often surprised to find out I had been born this way.

It's early days but there is no question that the Paralympics has helped take away some of those fears people had. It's removed the element of the unknown. The Games held disability up to the light and showed the extraordinary things disabled people can do. London told the world what I had always known – that we are world-class athletes in our own right.

Without a word of a lie, some people used to think that the wheelchair racers in the London Marathon had just got up that morning and decided to come along and race. It was so patronising. They didn't think we had trained all our lives to get to that start line. They assumed anyone in a wheelchair could get into a racing chair and become the next Tanni Grey-Thompson. That's like saying anyone can pull on a pair of running shoes and go out and beat Mo Farah. You have to have talent and you have to work extremely hard in training, day in, day out. A lot of those perceptions were changing. The coverage of our races in the London Marathon had started that process. What the Paralympics did was to put a rocket booster under all that.

I knew the Games had made a big breakthrough on the first night I raced, when I saw the Olympic Stadium sold out. And when it went on day after day and night after night with full house after full house, I just thought, 'Wow. What we have achieved here is incredible.'

All right, so I am sure that some of the people who came just wanted to come to the Olympic Park because they might not have been able to get tickets for the Olympics. And the prices were obviously a bit cheaper than the Olympics. But the organisers weren't giving them away. People still had to part with their hard-earned money to come and support us and I really appreciated that. Things are tough in the economy for people at the moment and I never took what they did lightly. And anyway, once they were there, the support they gave us was on a level I had never seen or heard before. For the first time in my life Paralympians were being treated as equal to able-bodied athletes. We weren't being watched out of pity or sympathy. We were being watched because we were the best at what we do. I never thought I would see that.

The day after I won my fourth gold medal I had to be up early again to get across the city to Guildhall and the start of the Heroes Parade. I know open-top bus parades with winning teams are pretty commonplace these days, but this one felt very different. More than 800 members of Team GB and Paralympics GB were involved. We were to be carried around on twenty-one floats in front of a crowd of hundreds of thousands of people. The route started in the City and wound its way along to Fleet Street and the Strand, then into Trafalgar Square before ending up on the Mall. As we waited to get on board the giant trucks I was doing interview after interview with people asking me how I felt. It was such a whirlwind. Great Olympians like Sir Ben Ainslie and Sir Chris Hoy were coming up to me and congratulating me on what I had achieved. That had never happened before. For the first time we were all one big group, one team.

Equals.

I was pretty late getting onto the back of my float because I was constantly being stopped by people asking for autographs. That was another new one for me. At one stage I had about thirty people queuing up and people passing things up for me to sign. I was on the same float as

Jessica Ennis. That was a real buzz. That's when she told me that I was her mum's second favourite athlete in the whole Games. When we finally set off and saw the scale of the crowds, it just blew me away. People hanging out of windows, standing on the top of bus shelters, howling like werewolves (a few even had the masks). It went on for about two and a half hours – it was so slow because there were so many people and so many trucks. I just thought, 'Look at what we have done to this country. This proves how powerful sport can be.'

Throughout the entire Games I hadn't heard one negative comment from a foreign athlete. Usually you hear someone moaning about something. I have done it myself when I have gone to other Games. But in London I didn't hear a single bad word. That made me so proud of my country.

But for the first time I was also really proud of the Paralympic movement and the way Seb Coe and the organising committee always made us feel part of the entire show. We weren't an afterthought. We were a main event in our own right. We had put ourselves on the world map as great sportspeople.

I think C4's coverage helped us turn that corner. The BBC had always done a great job for the Paralympics but showing our Games on a different channel made a massive difference. It was all C4 had to focus on whereas the BBC had to cover the Olympics. No matter what they said it might have left us feeling like the bridesmaid. That couldn't happen with C4. They were free to concentrate solely on us and they did a fantastic job in promoting and projecting our sports.

I loved the attitude. Their use of Public Enemy's 'Harder Than You Think' as their theme music was a stroke of genius. It totally summed it up. And the film that went with it was brilliant. It really challenged people's perceptions from the start. The film highlighted the everyday nature of being disabled – it can happen to anyone. A car crash, a misfortune of birth. It was very powerful. It was like I had always thought – that people shouldn't be afraid to ask difficult questions. This was the truth, why hide it? This is what it is.

It was the same with their use of humour. I loved *The Last Leg*, hosted by Adam Hills, although I have to admit I didn't watch it much until after the Games. The only time I actually watched it during the Paralympics was the night before the marathon because the hotel we were staying in had TVs in the bedroom. I know Adam and the team got a lot of bad comments at the beginning but slowly people warmed up to it and realised disabled people do take the piss out of each other. We are like everyone else. It's what we do. I also liked the fact that some of the reporters out at the events were disabled. Sometimes when you watch some shows you see disabled reporters and it feels like they are only there because of their condition. It wasn't like that in the Paralympics.

C4 also understood that the Paralympic athletes needed

to be introduced over a longer period of time than the Olympians. Jess Ennis, Bradley Wiggins and so on – they were household names already. But we needed publicity. We needed commercials and programmes to explain the classifications and the different sports. No one had really heard of blind football, goalball and boccia but C4 put them in the spotlight. They used an ex-wheelchair athlete to really explain to the audience how the racing chair worked and how athletes used different styles and techniques for various different distances and disciplines. Without that the Paralympics could have been bewildering. There are so many classifications and sports. So C4 introduced LEXI, a really simple system which explained each event and classification to people. They used illustrations which showed exactly which areas of the body were impaired and how severely. For example, my classification, the T54, is for athletes with moderate or severe impairment of the lower limbs. So it covers a wide range – from people like me who can't move their legs to those who have lost one or both legs. C4 used colour coding which was really clear and they did a great job of making the Paralympics more accessible. After all, it's not like running, where you can put on a pair of running shoes and off you go.

Inevitably, as time has gone on, I have started to question whether the Paralympics has made the difference everyone said it did. The truth is it's probably too early to judge.

Some experts argue that the Paralympics might have had a negative impact on people with disability in Britain. A lot of disabled people are facing cuts to welfare benefits and being told to stop scrounging and find a job. So the image of all these super-fit, gold-medal-winning athletes maybe undermined those people who genuinely need support. Maybe the critics have a point. Not everyone can be Jonnie Peacock and if people are on benefits they are on benefits for a reason.

But I can also see the other point of view. When I was younger I needed benefits. It was harder to get a job back then. People never looked beyond the wheelchair. Now, with the Equality Act, there's a big difference. The disabled person stands a chance in the workplace. If people can't work then they need to explain it.

On a more personal level I have to admit I have felt a bit let down by the way things have gone since the Paralympic flame went out. I don't want anyone to think I am hard done by. Let's be clear – London 2012 was first and foremost about winning. It wasn't about getting rich. And in the year since the Games I have done well from sponsorship deals with companies like BMW and GlaxoSmithKline.

BMW have been a great supporter. Not only have they provided me with a car, they have adapted it so I can drive it. It's actually much simpler than you think. It's an automatic car with a special lever installed which connects to the accelerator and the brake. If I want to accelerate I push in one direction. If I want to brake, then I pull it towards me. Simple as that. It's a great piece of technology which has transformed my life – especially with wheelchair racing.

You have to get your day chair and your racing chair around and there is so much other kit to carry. I currently have an X5 but I will soon be getting an X6. We need a bit of extra room with all the children now too.

I can also count on the support of the billionaire Topshop owner, Sir Philip Green. He has been helping me since 2009 through personal donations. It must be one of the luckiest things that has ever happened to me. It all started about five or six years ago. I was training in Richmond Park when a bloke walking his dog came up to me. He was called Randall and he explained that he used to work on the Stock Exchange but had since retired. He said he had a wealthy friend who might be interested in helping me. I gave him my number and never expected to hear another word. But sure enough Randall called back a couple of weeks later and told me about his connection to Sir Philip. He told me he was going to have a word with him.

Again, I didn't expect anything to come of it but a few weeks later Randall said Sir Philip and his wife had agreed to help me. They didn't want any publicity from it. They just wanted to help. And so, a few years later, Sir Philip started giving me an annual donation to help with my training. And to think I hadn't even met him at that point. After the Games I was inundated with requests from journalists. Because the Games had been so busy I hadn't had much of a chance to really open up and tell my side of the story. It had all been quick clips and press conferences. I wanted to do something once it had all died down but didn't know where to do it. So Sir Philip kindly agreed to step in and lend me one of his offices to hold a big media day.

The money from Sir Philip and my other deals has made me more comfortable than ever before. I no longer need to rely on National Lottery funding, and for a Paralympian that is quite a breakthrough. It's changed my life.

But people shouldn't imagine that I am now some high-rolling millionaire. People see me on the TV at this or that event and think I am now minted. But I still rent the same two-bedroom house from Sutton Council that I have lived in for more than a decade. In fact, as I write this, I am involved in a row with them about trying to swap my place for a bigger house with an extra bedroom. Once, a reporter from the *Daily Mail* phoned up to arrange an interview with Emily and when she told them roughly where we lived the journalist immediately assumed we lived in one of the big houses up in Purley. They were shocked when she told them to meet her at the Phoenix Leisure Centre on the Roundshaw Estate. My ambition is to eventually buy whichever council house we end up with so I can at least have a bit of an investment for my family. Something to build on.

In common with quite a few Olympians and Paralympians, my success in London didn't lead to a new kit sponsor. No Nike or Adidas came knocking on my door – despite winning four gold medals. You have to wonder what you have to do. My agent, Jamie Baulch, has been working his heart out to try and get me a kit deal and there are people out there saying they will give me free kit. But I am worth more than that. Maybe it's the wheelchair – because other Paralympians like Jonnie Peacock have managed to get deals. Maybe, at thirty-four, I'm simply too old.

The other thing that hasn't changed is the appearance and prize money from racing. When it comes to that, we are still a long way from being equal with the able-bodied athletes. I got double what I was paid for the marathon in 2012. But Mo Farah got at least ten times the amount I received for running half the race. I am not criticising the London Marathon guys. They have always been so supportive. I am simply pointing out the massive gap which exists.

The Anniversary Games in London is another good example. I was offered $7,000 to compete. Again, it's nice money and I wouldn't miss the chance to go back to that stadium for the world. But that fee was the same regardless of who you were or how many Paralympic gold medals you had won. I bet Jessica Ennis wasn't getting that amount.

I guess you have to accept it will never change. I thought what we did in the Games might have made a difference when it came to money. But it hasn't. I know some people might think I sound bitter. I'm not. I am doing very nicely and I can now look after my family in a way I couldn't have possibly imagined when I started competing all those years ago. I am simply saying that we shouldn't just swallow it when people say it changed everything. Yes, it shifted people's perceptions about the disabled. But we are a long way from being sporting equals.

I honestly don't know how some of the other Paralympic athletes keep going. It can only be through sheer hard work. That's one of the reasons I have set up the Weir Archer Academy with Jenny to try to help develop the next generation. I was lucky to have parents who both had jobs and had the money to support me. But not everyone with talent is that lucky, so I want the academy to try to help young aspiring athletes who aren't as lucky as I was.

The Weir Archer Academy officially opened on 6 April 2013. But it had been many years in the planning. After I came back from Beijing in 2008 I spoke to Jenny about doing something which would give disabled people the chance to play sport. I knew from my own experience how it had transformed my life. But I was also aware that it was hard for people to find the right facilities, kit and coaching. So Jenny and I started working on what a new academy for disability sport might look like. But for years it was nothing more than a pipe dream. All talk. I was so busy training and Jenny was so busy coaching me that it was another three years before it really started to take shape.

The fact that the dream has been realised is thanks in no small part to one of Jenny's oldest friends and fellow coaches, Camilla Thrush. She sat us down one day and asked us to spell out exactly what it was we wanted to do. She knew us both well enough to understand that unless we set it up properly then it wouldn't work. We would set out with good intentions and try to mark out time to work with all these new athletes but in the end it would probably fail. It had to be set up as a well-planned business, with funding and support in place and a team of staff and coaches to run the place.

We never imagined it would become what it is today.

The academy covers ten different sports, including wheelchair rugby and tennis, boccia, football, badminton and volleyball. Although it was set up with athletics in mind, it's not only about track and field. We recognise that to get more disabled people playing sport we have to create more opportunities in all sports.

We are hoping to support 5,500 people between the ages of ten and twenty-five in year one, rising to three times that number in 2016. It's a huge undertaking and the sums of money involved are pretty big. We are looking to raise about £1.4 million to cover the coaching and staffing costs by year three.

A lot of that money is coming from grants from Sport England, the agency which distributes lottery funds for Olympic and Paralympic legacy projects, but also from the Greater London Authority and the governing bodies that run the sports we are supporting.

But the academy is also driving a big refurbishment of Kingsmeadow, where I have spent so many years training and working on my sporting career. It's still in the design stages but I am hoping the £6.5 million project will leave us with new facilities and a sports centre dedicated to disabled sport.

A lot of the focus is inevitably on athletics and already we have seen a massive jump in numbers. In 2008 I was the only athlete Jenny coached. In 2012 she had eight. One year later, it's thirty-six. Sometimes the athletes are spotted by Jenny or recommended by another coach. But the majority of the group are people who have sent us emails asking us to help them. We have also had a couple of open training sessions which have been far more popular than I imagined. This has shown me first-hand the impact of the Paralympics.

Although the ambition is to develop the stars of tomorrow, I am also a firm believer that disabled people should be able to take part in sport just for fun and to keep fit. That's why the academy tries to help people of all abilities.

But I would really hope that by the time the Rio Paralympics come around in 2016 a few of the athletes from the academy are out there representing Great Britain. There are already some really promising athletes coming through: there's Jamie Carter, a 100m sprinter from Lincoln, who finished sixth in the T34 final in London – his first Paralympics. But I also have high hopes for Will Smith, who already races for GB, and Abbie Hunnisett, a club thrower who is third in the country but fifth overall in the world. If you actually look at my classification, T54, the academy has eleven of the top fifteen in the country.

Graham Spencer is only twelve but he is already one of the best in Britain. In fact, because of the way the classification system works, there's no minimum age requirement so he could actually race me now in competition.

The kids working with us now come from all over the country. The ones based in the south-east of England train with Jenny regularly on a Monday and Wednesday. Those from a bit further afield come down in the school holidays or at weekends. Jenny draws up a training programme for them and their parents to work with. She tells them what she told me all those years ago when she asked me to compete at the London Youth Games: 'Talent will get you so far, but I am looking for something else ... A bit of aggression and determination, something that marks you out from the rest. If you think this is going to be a fun factory, forget it.'

You see, the thing about Jenny is, she likes a challenge. She just gets such an amazing lift from helping kids fulfil their potential, regardless of where they come from or how much money they've got.

For me it's hard to get along to the academy as much as I would like. Although I train at Kingsmeadow all the time, I can only really devote one day a month to it. I would like to do a lot more and perhaps when I do finally pack up I will dedicate more time to helping the next generation.

One of the big aims of the academy is to help physical education teachers in schools to do more for disabled kids, so they aren't just sent to the library during games or PE lessons, as is so often the case. It's also quite hard for disabled children to do PE qualifications. There isn't that understanding in school, so we want to help the exam boards and schools learn how to assess people with disabilities.

My school understood the importance of sport to kids with disabilities but I am not always sure the mainstream schools get it. This academy didn't start off as a large-scale legacy project but over the next few years I am sure it will play a big part in ensuring the afterglow from the Paralympics doesn't just fade away.

———

After the Heroes Parade, I was finally able to get back home and to a bit of normality. Well, sort of. First I had a lads holiday in Ibiza to celebrate.

The truth is (and no one will believe me) I didn't really want to go. Emily was heavily pregnant – the baby could have come any day. But she just wanted me to be with my friends and enjoy myself for a few days. She made me go! So ten of us set off on one of those awful crack-of-dawn flights to Ibiza for five days. I'm glad I did. For nearly eighteen months I had just been focused on one thing. I had put everything else in my life on hold. Now I could let my hair down a bit. It was nice to be recognised by people out there while we were in some of the bars and clubs. And it was great to get the VIP treatment. But all the time I was phoning home, worried that I might miss the birth.

In the end I was back in good time – but that's not to say it was straightforward.

Tillia Grace London Weir was born at 11.30 p.m. on 7 October. In a new Weir record time of … twenty minutes.

Earlier that night we had gone up to St Helier Hospital because Emily had some pains. We waited for ages up there but the nurses said she wasn't dilated and sent us back home. The minute we pulled up outside the house she said, 'The baby is coming, the contractions have started.' She told me to drive to the hospital as fast I could. Halfway back to the hospital she suddenly said, 'Pull over. I think it's stopped.' I felt this wave of relief, and was just thinking about turning around when she started screaming again.

'Drive, drive.'

It's the nightmare you always thought would never happen to you. I was thinking, 'How the hell am I going to deliver a baby in my car?' So I was phoning the hospital trying to warn them and to get them to run the bath for the birth. Emily had hoped for a water birth, but in the end there was no time. As we rushed in I looked at the clock in the hospital reception. It had just gone 11 p.m. I did some calculations in my head and thought we would be out by 5 a.m. the next day.

After the midwife had checked Emily I asked her for a rough timing.

'About twenty minutes.'

'You have got to be joking?' And I looked down at Emily and there was Tilly's head already popping out. Before I knew it, she was here. No complications and no hitches. My beautiful baby girl. She was absolutely perfect and it felt like we had just popped to the shops and picked her up.

Coming up with the first part of our new arrival's name

was no problem. Emily and I had agreed on Tillia Grace a few weeks earlier. But I also wanted a name which would always remind her – and us – of the very special year she came along. I toyed with Gold or Goldie. Or even Weirwolf! Poor girl, can you imagine how she would have got teased at school? In the end, the answer was obvious: London.

My head was still spinning when the nurses told us we would soon be able to go home. It was just gone midnight and by 2 a.m. we were back in our house. It was unbelievable. It normally takes me longer to get through a drugs test after one of my races. Taking Tilly home was so special. 2012 had been such an incredible year. First the Paralympics and now a new baby. But, very quickly, the golden memories of London had to be put to one side as it was back to sleepless nights and changing nappies. Things became so hectic that there was absolutely no time to sit back and reflect.

It wasn't until Christmas and the BBC Sports Personality of the Year awards that I started to look back again at what I had done during those magical ten days. I know Bradley Wiggins said I deserved to win but I was just honoured to be on that list of twelve incredible athletes. I was also very proud that Ellie Simmonds and Sarah Storey were on the list too. To have three Paralympians out of twelve was a major leap forward. To come fifth in such an incredible year with contenders like Sir Chris Hoy and Sir Ben Ainslie behind me was an extraordinary achievement. I do think a Paralympian will win it one year. I just hope the BBC put us on there more regularly now we have made the break-through. It shouldn't just be because the BBC feel there should be a disabled athlete.

Then there was the New Year's Honours List. I know there was a bit of press that I was upset not to have got a knighthood. I don't know where that came from. I was making the point that I wasn't sure how the honours committee worked out who got what. But I was deeply honoured to get a CBE from the Queen. After all, I am only doing something I love. There are people who fight and die for their country and they don't even get a look in. We are ultimately doing something for fun.

———

Getting motivated to compete again after what had happened to me in London was always going to feel like a drag. For months I felt like I was on one giant victory lap, shuttling from reception to reception, awards do to awards do. With Tilly's arrival it left with me with no time to even think about racing or training. Besides, I was always going to take it easy over the winter, to let my body recuperate after the last couple of years.

By the spring of 2013 I was getting the itch to compete again. Fortunately, the London Marathon was just around the corner. After equalling Tanni Grey-Thompson's record of six wins in 2012, I told my brother that would be my last race. But after Christmas I changed my mind. I just wanted to see what it was like to be back on the streets of London. I wanted to know if the Paralympics really did change London and the country, if people would come out and cheer us. I was terrified it might all have been a one-off. Then there was the record. That seventh win. The one that would take me to a new level. Better even than the great Tanni Grey-Thompson. It was impossible to resist.

The build-up to that race was like nothing I had ever experienced before. The interest was massive. I had a news crew from Sky TV following me for eight weeks. And when I turned up on the Wednesday before the race at the marathon exhibition at the ExCeL Centre in London's Docklands, I had to be sneaked in through the back door. Every year for the last decade I have rolled in through the front. But this time there were so many camera crews and people there, the organisers decided it would probably be better if I just slipped in quietly through a back entrance. My mate Ricky came up with me and he couldn't believe what he was seeing. I don't think of myself as famous but I suppose I am. You just forget, and there were so many people wanting pictures. Even in the main press conference on the Friday there were loads of new faces asking me questions. Some of the regulars were there, people I have got to know down the years, but this year it was packed. Every channel and every paper was there. How did it feel to be confronted by all this? At times I felt awkward and uncomfortable. At others, proud and relaxed. If I am honest, the whole thing was crazy.

The biggest downside was the amount of time it all took. Spending four hours in a press conference two days before your big comeback is not exactly very smart. But you have to make the most of the attention while it is there. It may never happen again.

When I lined up on the start line on the Sunday, it felt great to be back in my chair. When the announcer read my name out, there was a massive roar – far louder than in previous years. And once the race was under way, the cheers and support seemed to be much bigger. I have never heard so many people shout my name. The weather was surprisingly warm and sunny and a combination of that and the Olympics had drawn one of the biggest crowds ever for a London Marathon. In some places it was six or seven deep. And there was definitely more recognition for the Brits. And apart from Mo Farah, who only did half the race, and me, there was no other British athlete who was in real contention to win. Maybe that's why there was more support for me that day. Whatever it was, it made for a very emotional afternoon.

Amidst all this chaos, I tried to keep my routine as normal as possible. Although the organisers booked me a room at a hotel right next to the Tower of London for four days, I only ever use the room for the night before the race. My brother picks me up from home and I actually drive myself to the start line. I have full-access passes to get through the streets. My brother then takes my car to the finish and I meet up with everyone there once I am done.

As with all big marathons the organisers arrange a bus for the athletes. But I don't like getting on that – someone's always late, or forgotten their gloves or helmet. I like to get there first thing and prepare in my own time. This time I had a few more friendly faces with me to give me support and even Emily came along, which was such a relief. Because what happened next didn't quite fit with the script I had written in my head.

Going into the race I felt in really good shape. But there's race fitness and there's training fitness. Halfway into the 26.2 miles I felt confident. But when some of the other athletes pushed on I was really fighting to stay in touch. I don't know if it was the pressure but it felt like I was hanging on for dear life. I didn't show it but inside I was struggling. I tried to lift myself but there was nothing there. I didn't have the right balance. I hadn't gone back to training until January and then the weather was so bad – we had snow two weeks before the marathon. That is unheard of. What it showed me was that the level of competition in wheelchair racing is getting higher all the time. You can't take time out and expect to just roll back in and win every-thing. It shows the strength and depth in my field and that you have to do your training. Some of the guys I was racing, they had been out in Dubai and warm-weather training. To compete you need to be out every day and some days a double session. Even in that short time between the end of the Games and the marathon I had fallen behind.

When Kurt Fearnley hit the front I had no answer. He

beat me comfortably and I could only manage fifth place. I was gutted. I looked for Emily at the finish line. She told me just to get my chin up. Then I saw Jenny. She put her arm around me (as she always does when I am down) and told me I had been through a crap winter and that I had to just move on. Having them there really saved me that day. I had wanted to win, to keep my unbelievable run in London going, but in the end my body wasn't up to it.

I suppose when you take all that into account finishing fifth wasn't disastrous. Ask any of the guys who beat me that day and I'm sure they would tell you they would have happily swapped their position in the 2013 marathon for one of my precious 2012 gold medals.

———

If the marathon gave me another taste of the London magic, then the Anniversary Games was like being transported back in time. Exactly one year on from the start of the Olympics, I was back in that beautiful Olympic Stadium. So much had happened to me in the twelve months since the Paralympics ended, but in the stadium time had stood still. Nothing had really changed. All right, so the Olympic and Paralympic cauldron had gone, along with the agitos, the Paralympic movement's answer to the Olympic rings. The place was decked out in the orange of sponsors Sainsbury's rather than the mauve of London 2012, but everything else looked the same – the same black and white seats, the same triangular floodlights and, most important of all, the same massive crowd. During the Paralympics and Olympics the capacity of the stadium was 80,000 but for the Anniversary Games it was scaled back to 60,000. But you could hardly tell the difference. The place was absolutely rammed and the atmosphere electric again. Over the course of two days of able-bodied athletics and then a single day of Paralympic track and field, British Athletics sold every available ticket. It was a great achievement and told me that we had made a real difference – that 2012 wasn't a one-off.

I wonder how it might be in ten years' time when the stadium is handed over to West Ham and they are playing in it every other week. How will it feel with retractable seats on the track, different floodlights and the Premier League club's claret and blue colours everywhere? My hope is that it will still ultimately have the same vibe, and in the end it's no good talking about creating a legacy and then not using the main stadium properly. The reality is that only football can really make use of that wonderful venue on a regular basis. As long as athletics is able to use it for its big meetings each year then I will be happy. I just pray they keep the track in good nick. I don't want it to be beaten up like the Stade de France in Paris. That used to be super-fast but it's not the same any more. They do too many events on it.

I was racing in a special invitational mile – a race set up by the organisers just for me to have a go at breaking the world record. It was scheduled right for the end – the climax to a nostalgic afternoon. At the start of the day I was asked to go out onto the track and do a little question-and-answer session with the announcer. While we were waiting to go on I suddenly realised that this was exactly the same area where we had had to wait before going to collect our medals. The same butterflies came rushing back. In fact, I felt more nervous. I never enjoy talking to crowds, let alone one 60,000 big. It was much worse than the nerves I get before any race. But they gave me an unbelievable reception.

Before the Anniversary Games I had been reading a lot of the stuff on Twitter. It was clear people were excited by the prospect of going back to the Olympic Park. Whether it was people who missed out on tickets in 2012 or others who did go and just wanted to relive those memories, I had absolutely no doubt that people would turn up. Unfortunately, when it came to my performance, the old Weirwolf didn't show. Although I was doing good times in training and felt OK, I wasn't race fit. I needed much more racing.

The funny thing is, in the weeks leading up to the race I followed exactly the same routine that I had set up in the run-up to 2012. I was back on the beetroot juice and doing the same kind of sessions in Richmond Park. But on the day I just couldn't seem to find that extra yard of pace I needed to do something really big. At the end, when I was interviewed by C4, you can see I was not very happy. I loved being cheered round again but I was disappointed with myself. I wanted to deliver a big finish for the crowd by breaking that record but in the end I couldn't do it.

If I was in a dark mood immediately after my race then it only got blacker once I tried to leave the stadium and meet up with Emily and the kids. I had already had a difficult journey there in the morning. British Athletics couldn't allocate me a parking space near the stadium so I had to dump the car in the Westfield shopping complex. All the Paralympians were in the same boat and I wasn't asking for special treatment but you have to ask whether Usain Bolt or any of the big stars of track and field would be asked to lug their kit across a packed shopping centre to pick up a bus from a hotel to take them to the stadium. I think I know the answer. I was already slightly flustered by a sudden change in the schedule – the organisers didn't tell me or my agent's representative, Mel Halling of Definitive, about the interview on the track before the meeting so I had left a bit later than normal just to concentrate on my race, which was three hours after the start. But now I had to be there much sooner. It really threw my preparations out as I like to be there in good time with everything tested and ready to go. Now I was rushing and I was irritated. Maybe that was one of the reasons why my race didn't go as well as I had hoped.

But none of that was as bad as what happened afterwards. Having jumped on the athletes' bus back to Westfield I was then dropped off at the entrance to the shopping centre to be confronted by thousands of fans drifting slowly away from the stadium. A lot of them were just making their way to the tube but some had stopped off for a drink or something to eat, and now here I was in the middle of a massive crowd. Don't get me wrong – it was absolutely lovely. People couldn't have been nicer. They only wanted autographs and to have a chat and pose for pictures. But it was also quite scary. I don't normally go into public areas immediately after my races so I wasn't used to it. The numbers were really big and I was landed right in the middle of it. The plan had been to find Emily and some other members of my family for a quick bite to eat but there was no way I was getting through. Luckily I was with Jenny, who was pushing Mason along behind me. He was fast asleep and so was completely oblivious to the mayhem around us. Then Mel, my agent's representative, spotted a couple of policemen. She explained the situation and, bless them, they gave us a police escort through the crowds. It was the first time I have ever been properly mobbed and to be honest it freaked me out. I felt bad that I couldn't sign everyone's piece of paper or T-shirt. Eventually, when I got through the crowd, I managed to meet up with Emily and a few friends and we did get something to eat. I was feeling quite shaky, though. Twelve months on, London 2012 still had the power to surprise.

———

Ask any of the British athletes involved in London 2012 – able bodied or disabled – and they will tell you it was just the most magical year. For Team GB and Paralympics GB to win so many golds and finish third in both medal tables was an incredible achievement. You always get a lift in a home Games and the crowd in Stratford obviously played a huge part in that. We also enjoyed record levels of funding, without which none of those marginal gains would have been possible.

What we have to do now is maintain those levels of funding. Even before the Games were over the government committed to keep the elite money at the same levels up until the Rio Olympics and Paralympics in 2016. That gives me a lot of confidence that we can repeat what we did in London when we get to Brazil. We have got enough funding now to stay there, and the talent's coming through. I don't see a dramatic drop or a return to the Atlanta days, when Great Britain won one Olympic gold medal in 1996. Sport is now much too important and is much better run than when I started. There is a lot of talk about legacy and I am sure there are loads of things we could do better but all the signs I see are good and the fact people are even talking about the L word tells me that we will keep pushing on as a sporting power.

As for my future, a lot of people keep asking about whether I will go on to Rio de Janeiro and the 2016 Paralympics. Even if my body can stand the sheer bloody torture of another three years of training – the cold, dark winters in Richmond Park followed by summers on the road competing – am I mentally up to it? Do I still have the drive to win, having achieved all my dreams in London?

Plus do I really want to give up all those hours with Emily and the kids?

Before London, the plan was clear: I would go for broke in 2012 and then look to bow out at the Commonwealth Games in Glasgow in 2014. I have never represented England and it felt like another big home Games would be the right moment to say goodbye. Beyond Glasgow I was very clear. I always thought, I'm not going to be one of those old stagers, still chasing the glory when they should have packed up years earlier. London would be my last shot at the big time. Once the flame went out that would be it, time to move on. Besides, I would be thirty-seven in Rio. Would people like Marcel have overtaken me by then? Would I really want to go to Brazil just to make up the numbers? That's not my style. If I put my name on a start list, I want to win.

But within a couple of weeks of London finishing I started to change my mind. Deep down I had always hoped, perhaps even expected, to win in London. But in the end I didn't just scrape home by the skin of my teeth – I blew the opposition away. No one really got close to me. Suddenly, London wasn't the end of my Paralympic journey. I knew I had a lot more to offer. Maybe I won't be able to go to Rio and win four golds again, but I am sure I can win at least one. If I manage that at the age of thirty-seven it will be a massive achievement. Even my performances in 2013 have given me confidence. The times might not be brilliant but no one has really been flying. I know I can still be a contender.

I had to tell Emily what was going through my head. In a few weeks' time we would have another baby to deal with and the impact on us as a family would be enormous. One night, I was sitting downstairs in the living room watching some TV. Emily was upstairs putting Mason to bed. My stomach flipped over as I prepared to deliver my bombshell.

'I am thinking about going to Rio,' I told her. At first she didn't say anything but I could tell she had been expecting something like this. 'So, what do you think?'

'I think you should definitely do it,' she said, smiling. 'In fact, I want you to do it.'

And that was that. No drama, no fuss. Decision made. We both smiled and I gave her a big cuddle. She had seen the way I won in London. Like me, she knew it was a game changer.

I also know that I won't be under the same sort of pressure that I faced in the build-up to London. Of course I will want to do well and win in Brazil, but I won't feel like I am carrying the world on my shoulders.

It was so nice for me to watch the 2013 World Championships in Lyon and see the team doing so well without me. Normally we have a bit of a dip after a Paralympics but this time there wasn't one. The British team won eleven gold medals. That showed we have some real strength in depth and that gives me a greater sense of freedom. But seeing the team do so brilliantly in France relit my competitive fire. It made me hungry to compete again at the highest level. I hadn't expected that. On Channel 4 the presenters kept trying to wind me up. Marcel Hug had a brilliant Championships and performed amazingly. As his medal count grew, they kept having little digs.

'I wonder if Dave Weir is watching?' they asked.

I tweeted my reply.

'Don't worry, I'm watching. I'll be back.'

DAVID WEIR:
A CAREER IN STATS

DOMESTIC RECORD

2013   Virgin London Marathon fifth

2012   Virgin London Marathon gold

2011   Virgin London Marathon gold

2010   Virgin London Marathon bronze

2009   Great North Run gold, Virgin London Marathon silver

2008   Great North Run gold

2007   Flora London Marathon gold

2006   Flora London Marathon gold

2005   Flora London Marathon gold

2004   Great North Run gold, Flora London Marathon bronze

2003   Great North Run gold, Flora London Marathon silver

2002   Flora London Marathon gold

MAJOR CHAMPIONSHIPS AND INTERNATIONAL RECORD

2012   Paralympics 800m gold, 1,500m gold, 5,000m gold, marathon gold. Swiss National Championships 5,000m gold, 800m silver, 1,500m sixth

2011   IPC Athletic Championships 800m gold, 1,500m gold, 5,000m gold

2010   ING New York City Marathon gold

2008   Paralympics 800m gold, 1,500m gold, 400m silver, 5,000m bronze

2007   Paralympic World Cup 400m gold, 1,500m gold

2006   European Championships (non-disabled) 1,500m gold

2006   World Championships 100m gold, 400m gold, 1,500m gold, 200m silver

2005   World Championships (non-disabled) 100m gold, 200m gold (demonstration events)

2005   European Championships 400m gold, 200m silver, 100m bronze

2004   Paralympics 100m silver, 200m bronze

1996   Paralympics 100m seventh, 4 x 100m relay fourth

DAVID WEIR'S CLASSIFICATION (ADAPTED FROM THE INTERNATIONAL PARALYMPIC COMMITTEE HANDBOOK)

T54 is for athletes competing in wheelchair racing events. T54 competitors have little or no impairment of their arm and shoulder functions – pertinent for pushing a wheelchair – but have partial trunk and leg function.

ACKNOWLEDGEMENTS

I owe thanks to so many people who have helped me in my racing career. Where do I start?

I have no doubt that without Jenny I wouldn't be where I am today, and I would not have been able to achieve everything that I have without her help and support. This is something I shall always be grateful to her for.

During my training pre-London 2012, Jenny introduced a team of cyclists. Included in the team are Alan and Stewart, and I would just like to take this opportunity to thank them for their hard work. They made me push my training regime to another level.

The Weir Archer Academy is my legacy: I simply want to pass on knowledge and experience to the next generation of disabled athletes. Our ambition is to work with other top-class coaches, and to support our staff to deliver their innovative, unsurpassed method to as many athletes as possible, from club to elite level. I would like to thank Camilla and Sam for making my dream a reality.

I would like to take this opportunity to thank my friends at St Mary's University for their support over the past few years; they know who they are.

I must also mention that without my sponsors I would not be able to follow my dream and compete at the level that I do today. Their support is invaluable.

I owe a great many thanks to the people behind this book: without them it would not have been possible. Thanks and appreciation to David Bond, who has worked with me to ensure that my story is told in my own way; to Charlie Campbell at Ed Victor; to the publishers, Biteback; and to my agents, Definitive Sports Management.

London 2012 was special. My Team GB mates, namely Dan Greaves and Aled Davies MBE, were with me every step of the way – quite simply, thanks boys!

My brothers and my friends are also very special people, very close to me. There are too many friends to mention individually, but they know who they are: thanks, guys, for always being there when it counts!

Finally, and most importantly, I would like to thank my fiancée, Emily. Without her encouragement, patience and love over the past few years I wouldn't be the man I am today. I also thank my mum and dad, Jackie and David, for their faith in me and for allowing me to follow my dream. It was under their watchful eye that I gained so much drive and ability to tackle challenges head on; thanks to them my dream was achieved.

DAVID BOND

David Bond is the BBC's sports editor and fronted BBC News's widely applauded coverage of the London 2012 Olympic and Paralympic Games. Before joining the BBC he was the sports editor of the *Daily Telegraph* and has also worked for the London *Evening Standard* and the *Sunday Times*. Over the last three years, he has covered the 2010 World Cup in South Africa, the FIFA corruption affair and cricket's spot-fixing. He has always focused on the stories behind sport – the movers and shakers who run the show; the big money deals; and the scandals which have come to shape and dominate what is, today, a multi-billion-pound business. David is forty, is married to Lucy, lives in south-west London and has two children, Max and Willow Clemency.

PICTURE CREDITS

Plate section

p. 3 top left © Gareth Fuller/LOCOG/Press Association Images

p. 4 top © MSgt Sean M. Worrell

p. 4 middle © Ed Clayton

p. 4 bottom © Caroline Granycome

p. 5 top © Teecefamily

p. 5 bottom ©Paul Ellis/AFP/GettyImages

p. 6 bottom left © Dominic Lipinski/PA Wire

p. 6 bottom right © John Stillwell/PA Wire

p. 7 top left © Elsie Kibue / Demotix/Demotix/Press Association Images

p. 7 top right © Steve Parsons/PA Wire

p. 7 bottom © Adam Davy/PA Wire

p. 8 top © Harry Engels/Getty Images

p. 8 bottom ©Jamie McDonald/Getty Images

INDEX

Available now from The Robson Press
COURT CONFIDENTIAL

Neil Harman

Tennis has never before been blessed with such an array of talented stars doing battle for the sport's most coveted titles. Games featuring Murray, Nadal, Federer, Djokovic, the Williams sisters and Maria Sharapova are among the most thrilling matches in the history of the game.

Court Confidential recounts a defining time for modern-day tennis: from Wimbledon to the Olympic Games, from Serena Williams's battle with illness to Andy Murray's historic grand slam victory, this is a book for tennis fans everywhere.

400pp hardback, £20
Available now in all good bookshops or order from
www.therobsonpress.com

Available now from Biteback Publishing
WAYNE ROONEY: BOOTS OF GOLD

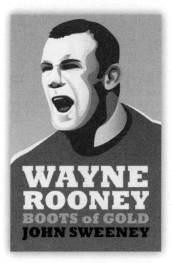

John Sweeney

Wayne Rooney: Boots of Gold is a tarts-and-all biography of England's most famous sportsman and an exposé of the iniquities of some of those who have sought their pound of flesh from his celebrity.

Short-tempered and sweary he may be, but there's no doubting Rooney's passion for the beautiful game. But who is the real Wayne Rooney? *Wayne Rooney: Boots of Gold* charts the rise and fall – and rise and fall again – of football's most intriguing star.

304pp paperback, £8.99
Available now in all good bookshops or order from
www.bitebackpublishing.com